A New Star-Rating System & Other Exciting News from Frommer's!

In our continuing effort to publish the savviest, most up-to-date, and most appealing travel guides available, we've added some great new features.

Frommer's guides now include a new **star-rating system.** Every hotel, restaurant, and attraction is rated from 0 to 3 stars to help you set priorities and organize your time.

We've also added **seven brand-new features** that point you to the great deals, in-the-know advice, and unique experiences that separate travelers from tourists. Throughout the guide, look for:

Finds	Special finds—those places only insiders know about
Fun Fact	Fun facts—details that make travelers more informed and their trips more fun
Kids	Best bets for kids—advice for the whole family
Moments	Special moments—those experiences that memories are made of
Overrated	Places or experiences not worth your time or money
Tips	Insider tips—some great ways to save time and money
Value	Great values—where to get the best deals

Here's what critics say about Frommer's:

"Amazingly easy to use. Very portable, very complete."

—Booklist

"Detailed, accurate, and easy-to-read information for all price ranges."

—Glamour Magazine

"Hotel information is close to encyclopedic."

—Des Moines Sunday Register

"Frommer's Guides have a way of giving you a real feel for a place."

—Knight Ridder Newspapers

Frommer's®

PORTABLE

Portland

2nd Edition

by Karl Samson & Jane Aukshunas

Wiley Publishing, Inc.

Published by:

WILEY PUBLISHING, INC.

909 Third Ave.
New York, NY 10022

ISBN 0-7645-6721-7
ISSN 1531-7528

Editor: Paul E. Kruger
Production Editor: Heather Wilcox
Photo Editor: Richard Fox
Cartographer: Roberta Stockwell
Production by Wiley Indianapolis Composition Services

For information on our other products and services or to obtain technical
support, please contact our Customer Care Department within the U.S. at
800-762-2974, outside the U.S. at 317-572-3993 or fax 317-572-4002.

Wiley also publishes its books in a variety of electronic formats. Some con-
tent that appears in print may not be available in electronic formats.

Manufactured in the United States of America

5   4   3   2

Contents

List of Maps

ABOUT THE AUTHORS

Husband-and-wife travel-writing team **Karl Samson** and **Jane Aukshunas** make their home in Oregon, where they spend their time juggling their obsessions with traveling, outdoor sports, and gardening. Each winter, to dry out their webbed feet, they flee the soggy Northwest to update the *Frommer's Arizona* guide, but they always look forward to their return to the land of good coffee. Karl is also the author of *Frommer's Great Outdoor Guide to Washington & Oregon* and *Frommer's Nepal*.

AN INVITATION TO THE READER

In researching this book, we discovered many wonderful places—hotels, restaurants, shops, and more. We're sure you'll find others. Please tell us about them, so we can share the information with your fellow travelers in upcoming editions. If you were disappointed with a recommendation, we'd love to know that, too. Please write to:

Frommer's Portable Portland, 2nd Edition
Wiley Publishing, Inc. • 909 Third Ave. • New York, NY 10022

AN ADDITIONAL NOTE

Please be advised that travel information is subject to change at any time—and this is especially true of prices. We therefore suggest that you write or call ahead for confirmation when making your travel plans. The authors, editors, and publisher cannot be held responsible for the experiences of readers while traveling. Your safety is important to us, however, so we encourage you to stay alert and be aware of your surroundings. Keep a close eye on cameras, purses, and wallets, all favorite targets of thieves and pickpockets.

WHAT THE SYMBOLS MEAN

The following abbreviations are used for credit cards:

AE	American Express	DISC	Discover	V	Visa
DC	Diners Club	MC	MasterCard		

FROMMERS.COM

Now that you have the guidebook to a great trip, visit our website at **www.frommers.com** for travel information on nearly 2,500 destinations. With features updated regularly, we give you instant access to the most current trip-planning information available. At Frommers.com, you'll also find the best prices on airfares, accommodations, and car rentals—and you can even book travel online through our travel booking partners. At Frommers.com, you'll also find the following:

- Online updates to our most popular guidebooks
- Vacation sweepstakes and contest giveaways
- Newsletter highlighting the hottest travel trends
- Online travel message boards with featured travel discussions

The Best of Portland

Situated at the confluence of the Willamette and Columbia Rivers, Portland, Oregon, with a population of roughly 1.8 million in the metropolitan area, is a city of discreet charms. That the city claims a rose garden as one of its biggest attractions should give you an idea of just how laid-back it is. Sure, Portlanders are just as attached to their cellphones and pagers as residents of other major metropolitan areas, but this is the City of Roses, and people still take time to stop and smell the flowers. Spend much time here, and you, too, will likely feel the city's leisurely pace seeping into your bones.

While nearby Seattle, Washington, has zoomed into the national consciousness, Portland has, until recently, managed to dodge the limelight and the problems that come with skyrocketing popularity. For many years now Portland has looked upon itself as a small, accessible city, vaguely European in character. *Clean* and *friendly* are the two terms that crop up most often in descriptions of the city. However, as word has spread about overcrowding in Seattle, people looking for the good life and affordable housing have turned to Portland, which is now experiencing the same sort of rapid growth that Seattle began going through more than a decade ago.

Portland does not have any major tourist sights. Instead, it is a city of quiet charms that must be searched for and savored—the shade of the stately elms in the South Park Blocks, the tranquillity of the Japanese Garden, the view from the grounds of Pittock Mansion, the miles of hiking trails in Forest Park. Sure, there's a good art museum and a world-class science museum, but these are not nearly as important to the city's citizenry as its many parks and public gardens. Not only does Portland claim beautiful rose gardens, the most authentic Japanese Garden in North America, and the largest classical Chinese garden in the country, but it also can lay claim to both the world's smallest city park and the largest forested urban park in the country.

The city's other claim to fame is as the nation's microbrew capital. Espresso may be the beverage that gets this town going in the morning (this *is* the Northwest), but it is microbrewed beer that helps the city maintain its mellow character. There are so many brewpubs here in Portland that the city has been nicknamed Munich on the Willamette. Wine is also popular, which shouldn't come as a surprise, considering how close the city is to wine country.

Portland itself may be short on things for visitors to do, but the city's surroundings certainly are not. Within a 1½- to 2-hour drive from Portland, you can be strolling on a Pacific Ocean beach, walking beside a waterfall in the Columbia Gorge, hiking on Mount Hood (a dormant volcano as picture perfect as Mt. Fuji), driving through the Mount St. Helens blast zone, or sampling world-class Pinot Noirs in the Oregon wine country. It is this proximity to the outdoors that makes Portland a great city to use as a base for exploring some of the best of the Northwest.

1 Frommer's Favorite Portland Experiences

- **Strolling the Grounds at the Japanese Garden.** This is the best Japanese Garden in the United States, perhaps the best anywhere outside of Japan. Our favorite time to visit is in June when the Japanese irises are in bloom. There's no better stress-reducer in the city.

- **Beer Sampling at Brewpubs.** They may not have invented beer here in Portland, but they certainly have turned it into an art form. Whether you're looking for a cozy corner pub or an upscale taproom, you'll find a brewpub where you can feel comfortable sampling what local brewmeisters are concocting.

- **Kayaking Around Ross Island.** Seattle may be considered the sea kayaking capital of the Northwest, but Portland's not a bad spot for pursuing this sport either. You can paddle on the Columbia or Willamette River, but our favorite easy paddle is around Ross Island in the Willamette River. You can even paddle past the submarine at the Oregon Museum of Science and Industry and pull out at Tom McCall Waterfront Park.

- **Mountain Biking the Leif Ericson Trail.** Forest Park is the largest forested city park in the country, and running its length is the unpaved Leif Ericson Road. The road is closed to cars and extends for 12 miles. Along the way, there are occasional views of the Columbia River. This is a pretty easy ride, without any strenuous climbs.

- **Driving and Hiking in the Gorge.** No matter what time of year it is, the drive up the Columbia Gorge is spectacular.

There are dozens of easily accessible hiking trails throughout the gorge. If you've got time to spare, take the scenic highway; if not, take I-84. No matter which road you take, be sure to pull off at Multnomah Falls. For an alternative point of view, drive the Washington side of the river and stop to hike to the top of Beacon Rock.

- **Hiking and Skiing on Mount Hood.** Less than an hour from Portland, Mount Hood offers year-round skiing and hiking. Timberline Lodge, high on this dormant volcano's slopes, was built by the WPA during the Great Depression and is a showcase of craftsmanship.

- **Hanging Out at Powell's.** They don't call Powell's the City of Books for nothing. This bookstore, which sells both new and used books, is so big you have to get a map at the front door. No matter how much time we spend here, it's never enough. A large cafe makes it all that much easier to while away the hours.

- **Free Rides on the Vintage Trolleys.** Tri-Met buses and MAX light-rail trolleys are all free within a large downtown area known as the Fareless Square. That alone should be enough to get you on some form of public transit while you're in town, but if you're really lucky, you might catch one of the vintage trolley cars. There aren't any San Francisco–style hills, but these old trolley cars are still fun to ride.

- **People-Watching at Pioneer Courthouse Square.** This is the heart and soul of downtown Portland, and no matter what time of year or what the weather, people gather here. Grab a latte at the Starbucks and sit by the waterfall fountain. In summer, there are concerts here, both at lunchtime and in the evenings; and any time of year you might catch a rally, performance, or installation of some kind. Don't miss the *Weather Machine* show at noon.

- **An Afternoon at the Portland Saturday Market.** This large arts-and-crafts market is an outdoor showcase for hundreds of the Northwest's creative artisans. You'll find fascinating one-of-a-kind clothes, jewelry, kitchenware, musical instruments, and much, much more. The food stalls serve up some great fast food, too.

- **Concerts at the Schnitz.** The Arlene Schnitzer Concert Hall, home to the Oregon Symphony, is a restored 1920s movie palace and is the city's most impressive place to attend a performance. Even if the show doesn't meet your expectations, you can enjoy the classic architectural details.

- **Summertime Concerts at the Washington Park Zoo.** Summertime in Portland means partying with the pachyderms. Two to three evenings a week throughout the summer, you can catch live music at the zoo's amphitheater. Musical styles include blues, rock, bluegrass, folk, Celtic, and jazz. For the price of zoo admission, you can catch the concert and tour the zoo (if you arrive early enough). Picnics are encouraged, but no alcohol is allowed into the zoo (however, beer and wine are on sale during concerts).
- **Summer Festivals at Waterfront Park.** Each summer, Tom McCall Waterfront Park, which stretches along the Willamette River in downtown Portland, becomes the staging ground for everything from Rose Festival events to the Oregon Brewers Festival. Some festivals are free and some have small cover charges, but all are lots of fun.
- **First Thursday Art Walk.** On the first Thursday of every month, Portland goes on an art binge. People get dressed up and go gallery hopping from art opening to art opening. There are usually hors d'oeuvres and wine available, and sometimes there's even live music. The galleries stay open until 9pm.

2 Best Hotel Bets

- **Best Historic Hotel:** With its sepia-tone murals of Lewis and Clark on the lobby walls and comfortable overstuffed leather chairs by the fireplace, the **Governor Hotel,** 611 SW 10th Ave. (© **800/554-3456** or 503/224-3400), built in 1909, captures both the spirit of the Northwest and the luxury of a classic hotel in both its public areas and its guest rooms.
- **Best for Business Travelers:** With fax machines in every room, plenty of room for spreading out your work, a convenient business center, a good restaurant, a day spa, and evening wine tastings, the **5th Avenue Suites Hotel,** 506 SW Washington St. (© **800/711-2971** or 503/222-0001), has everything necessary to make a business trip both successful and enjoyable.
- **Best for a Romantic Getaway:** If you're looking for the most romantic room in town, book a starlight room at the **Hotel Vintage Plaza,** 422 SW Broadway (© **800/243-0555** or 503/228-1212). Located on one of the hotel's upper floors, these rooms are basically solariums with curving walls of glass that let you lie in bed and gaze up at the stars. Just be sure

to come in the summer when there aren't as many clouds in the sky.

- **Best Lobby for Pretending That You're Rich:** With its walnut paneling, Italian marble, and crystal chandeliers, **The Benson,** 309 SW Broadway (© 800/426-0670 or 503/228-2000), is the pinnacle of 19th-century elegance. Order a snifter of brandy, sink into one of the leather chairs by the fireplace, and you too can conjure up your past life as a railroad baron.

- **Best for Families:** Although it is located in Vancouver, Washington, 20 minutes from downtown Portland, the **Homewood Suites Hotel Vancouver/Portland,** 701 SE Columbia Shores Blvd. (© **800/CALL-HOME** or 360/750-1100), is a good bet for families. Guest rooms are more like apartments, and rates include breakfast and a big spread of evening appetizers. There's also a 5-mile-long paved riverside trail across the street.

- **Best Moderately Priced Hotel:** Although it is totally unassuming from the outside, the **Four Points Hotel Sheraton,** 50 SW Morrison Ave. (© **800/899-0247** or 503/221-0711), with its very contemporary interior decor, is one of Portland's most stylish hotels. Add to this the fact that Waterfront Park and the Willamette River are just across the street, and you've got a great deal (if you can reserve far enough in advance to get a low rate).

- **Best Inexpensive Hotel:** How about a waterfront motel in Portland's most prestigious suburb for under $80? Try the **Lakeshore Inn,** 210 N. State St., Lake Oswego (© **800/215-6431** or 503/636-9679), a small motel right on the lake, with a swimming pool on a dock. The catch is that it's 7 miles from downtown Portland.

- **Best B&B:** With views, attractive gardens, a secluded feel, and the shops, restaurants, and cafes of NW 23rd Avenue only blocks away, the **Heron Haus,** 2545 NW Westover Rd. (© **503/274-1846**), is Portland's most luxurious and conveniently located B&B.

- **Best Service:** Though quite unpretentious, the historic **Heathman Hotel,** 1001 SW Broadway (© **800/551-0011** or 503/241-4100), is one of Portland's finest hotels and is long on personal service.

- **Best Location:** Though it's only a few blocks from downtown businesses, the **RiverPlace Hotel,** 1510 SW Harbor Way (© **800/227-1333** or 503/228-3233), a boutique hotel wedged between the Willamette River and Tom McCall Riverfront Park, feels a world away from the city. In summer, the park hosts countless festivals and if you book the right room, you can have a box seat for a concert in the park.

- **Best Health Club:** If you stay at the **Governor Hotel,** 611 SW 10th Ave. (© **800/554-3456** or 503/224-3400), you need only head down to the basement for a total workout at the Princeton Athletic Club. For $8 a day, you can use the lap pool, running track, exercise room, whirlpool spas, saunas, and steam rooms.

- **Best Views:** So, you've seen that photo of the Portland skyline with Mount Hood in the distance and you want that view while you're in town. Sorry, you'll have to sleep in Washington Park for that one. But the next best bet is an east-side room on an upper floor of the **Portland Marriott Downtown,** 1401 SW Naito Pkwy. (© **800/228-9290** or 503/226-7600).

- **Best West-Side Hotel:** If you're here on high-tech business in the Beaverton/Hillsboro area or just prefer a little greenery around you, there is no better choice than the **Greenwood Inn,** 10700 SW Allen Blvd. (© **800/289-1300** or 503/643-7444). This resortlike hotel has a great restaurant, fun lounge, and very attractive rooms, and all only 15 minutes from downtown Portland.

- **Best for Travelers with Disabilities:** Located right in the heart of downtown, on the bus mall, the **Embassy Suites,** 319 SW Pine St. (© **800/EMBASSY** or 503/279-9000), is an excellent choice for any traveler restricted to a wheelchair. Most of the rooms here are suites, which means you won't have to deal with a cramped hotel room. The location in the heart of downtown also puts you close to all of Portland's main downtown attractions.

- **Best Uncategorizable Hotel:** What can you say about a hotel that's located in a renovated poor farm and has a brewery, winery, distillery, movie theater, and golf course? Cheers! At **McMenamins Edgefield,** 2126 SW Halsey St., Troutdale (© **800/669-8610** or 503/669-8610), on the eastern edge of the Portland Metro area, a local brewpub empire has produced one of the most unusual lodgings in the state. The affiliated **McMenamins Kennedy School,** 5736 NE 33rd Ave. (© **888/249-3983** or 503/249-3983), is very similar and closer in.

3 Best Dining Bets

- **Best Spot for a Romantic Dinner:** With dramatic lighting, dark corners, sensuous food, and superb wines, **Assaggio,** 7742 SE 13th Ave. (© **503/232-6151**), a neighborhood trattoria in the Sellwood district, is a sure bet for a romantic dinner.
- **Best Place to Close a Deal: The London Grill,** 309 SW Broadway (© **503/228-2000**), at the Benson Hotel, a hotel favored by presidents and other power lunchers, is an unparalleled place for conducting business.
- **Best Spot for a Celebration:** With a decor that harkens back to the days of fin-de-siècle Paris, **Brasserie Montmartre,** 626 SW Park Ave. (© **503/224-5552**), has live jazz and a performing magician several nights a week. Plus, your entire party can color all over the (paper) tablecloths with crayons.
- **Best Decor:** If contemporary decor appeals to you, **Wildwood,** 1221 NW 21st Ave. (© **503/248-WOOD**), one of the anchors of NW 21st Avenue's Restaurant Row, is the place. The hard-edged interior is straight out of *Architectural Digest.*
- **Best Wine List:** You can sample some of the best wines around at **Paley's Place,** 1204 NW 21st Ave. (© **503/243-2403**). The food here is vibrantly flavorful Northwest and French-inspired cuisine.
- **Best Value:** If you happen to be a frugal gourmet whose palate is more sophisticated than your wallet can afford, you'll appreciate the **Western Culinary Institute International Dining Room,** 1316 SW 13th Ave. (© **503/294-9770** or 800/ 666-0312), where a five-course lunch will set you back only about $8 (reservations required).
- **Best for Kids: The Old Spaghetti Factory,** 0715 SW Bancroft St. (© **503/222-5375**), may not serve the best Italian food in town, but it certainly is some of the cheapest, and the waterfront location and eclectic decor are a hit with kids and parents alike.

- **Best Gourmet Fast Food:** It's just a tiny place, but **Ken's Home Plate,** 1852 SE Hawthorne Blvd. (© 503/236-9520), is crammed full of irresistible goodies to stay or to go. There's another Ken's Home Plate in the Pearl District at 1208 NW Glisan St. (© **503/517-8935**).
- **Best French: Couvron,** 1126 SW 18th Ave. (© **503/ 225-1844**), a tiny cottage French restaurant not far from downtown, serves the most eclectic and creative French and French-influenced meals in the city.
- **Best Northwest:** The **Heathman Restaurant and Bar,** SW Broadway at Salmon St. (© **503/790-7758**), at the elegant Heathman Hotel, features the very best Northwest meat, seafood, wild game, and produce, all with a French accent.
- **Best Mexican:** With an outpost on either side of the river, **Chez José East,** 2200 NE Broadway (© **503/280-9888**), serves the most creative and unusual Mexican food in the city. It's not what you'd expect from a Mexican restaurant, which is exactly what makes it so good.
- **Best Seafood:** Get 'em while they're hot at **Jake's Famous Crawfish,** 401 SW 12th Ave. (© **503/226-1419**). Crawfish are the stars of the menu here, and have been for years, but you can also get lots of other fresh seafood.
- **Best Pizza:** Portland's best pizza (crispy crusts and creative ingredients) can be found at the numerous **Pizzicato Gourmet Pizza** restaurants around the city. The downtown outpost is at 705 SW Alder St. (© **503/226-1007**).
- **Best Desserts: Papa Haydn West,** 701 NW 23rd Ave. (© **503/ 228-7317**), offers a symphony that includes lemon chiffon torte, raspberry gâteau, and Irish coffee Charlotte, to name but a few. There's usually a line at the door, but don't let that deter you. There's another location at 5829 SE Milwaukie Ave. (© **503/232-9440**) in Sellwood.
- **Best Outdoor Dining:** You just can't get any closer to the river than the **Newport Bay Restaurant,** 0425 SW Montgomery St. (© **503/227-3474**), which is in a floating building in the marina at Portland's RiverPlace shopping-and-dining complex. The Newport Bay provides excellent views of the river and the city skyline, especially from the deck.
- **Best Brunch:** The most lavish brunch in Portland is served at The Benson Hotel's **London Grill,** 309 SW Broadway (© **503/ 228-2000**), located downstairs from the marble-floored lobby.

2

Planning Your Trip to Portland

One of your first considerations when planning your trip should be when to visit. Summer is the peak season in the Northwest, the season for sunshine and outdoor festivals and events. During the summer months, hotel and car reservations are almost essential; the rest of the year they're highly advisable but not nearly as imperative. Keep in mind, however, that when booking a plane, hotel, or rental car, you can usually get better rates by reserving weeks in advance.

1 Visitor Information

For information on Portland and the rest of Oregon, contact the **Portland Oregon Visitors Association (POVA),** 1000 SW Broadway, Suite 2300, Portland, OR 97205 (© **877/678-5263** or 503/275-9750; www.travelportland.com). See also "Visitor Information" in chapter 3, "Getting to Know Portland."

If you're surfing the Net, you can also get additional Portland information at the following websites: *Willamette Week* (**www.wweek.com**), Portland's arts and entertainment weekly, or *The Oregonian* (**www.oregonian.com**), Portland's daily newspaper.

2 Money

ATMs can be found at banks, convenience stores, in many night-clubs, at the Saturday Market, at festivals (portable machines), and other locations around the city. Expect to pay a $1.50 service charge if you use an ATM that is not affiliated with your own bank, in addition to what your home bank charges. The most common ATM networks are Star, Cirrus, PLUS, Accel, and the Exchange.

ATMs have made **traveler's checks** all but obsolete. Although they're generally accepted at most restaurants, hotels, and shops in neighborhoods frequented by tourists, such as downtown and Nob Hill, they're not nearly as widely accepted as credit cards.

At most banks, you can get a cash advance with your credit card at the ATM if you know your PIN number.

Almost every credit-card company has an emergency toll-free number that you can call if your wallet or purse is stolen. The toll-free information directory will provide the number if you dial 🕿 800/555-1212. **Citicorp Visa**'s U.S. emergency number is 🕿 800/336-8472. **American Express** cardholders and traveler's check holders should call 🕿 800/221-7282 for all money emergencies. **MasterCard** holders should call 🕿 800/307-7309.

3 When to Go

While summer is the sunniest season in Portland, and the obvious time to visit, it's also the most crowded time of year. Although the city is not yet so popular that you can't usually get a room in town at the last minute, you'll definitely have more choices if you plan ahead. If, on the other hand, you visit in one of the rainier months, between October and May, you'll find lower hotel room rates and almost as much to see and do.

THE WEATHER

This is the section you've all been looking for. You've all heard about the horrible weather in the Northwest. It rains all year, right? Wrong! The Portland area has some of the most beautiful summer weather in the country—warm, sunny days with clear blue skies and cool nights perfect for sleeping. During July, August, and September, it almost never rains.

And the rest of the year? Well, yes, it rains in those months and it rains regularly. But the rain is generally a fine mist—not the torrential downpours most people associate with the word rain. The average annual rainfall in Portland is less than it is in New York, Boston, Washington, D.C., or Atlanta (but Portland has more days of rain and more cloudy days). A raincoat and a sweater or jacket are all a way of life in this part of the country, with Gore-Tex the preferred material. Portlanders seldom use umbrellas since the rain is rarely more than a steady drizzle.

Winters here aren't too bad, either. They're warmer than in the Northeast, although there is snow in nearby mountains. In fact, there's so much snow on Mount Hood—only 90 minutes from downtown Portland—that you can ski right through the summer.

All in all, the best months to visit are August and September, and if you're headed to the coast, September is definitely the best month.

Octobers can be very pleasant if the rainy season starts slowly. Even in the spring there are often weeks, here and there, when the sun shines, and even when it doesn't, the spring flower displays around Portland are so colorful that you hardly notice that the skies are gray.

Of course you're skeptical, so here are the statistics.

Portland's Average Temperature & Days of Rain

	Jan	Feb	Mar	Apr	May	June	July	Aug	Sept	Oct	Nov	Dec
Temp. (°F)	40	43	46	50	57	63	68	67	63	54	46	41
Temp. (°C)	4	6	8	10	14	17	20	19	17	12	8	5
Rain (Days)	18	16	17	14	12	10	4	5	8	13	18	19

PORTLAND CALENDAR OF EVENTS

For a calendar of special events in and around Portland, contact the **Portland Oregon Visitors Association** (see section 1 of this chapter, above), which lists special events in a couple of its publications and also on its website (**www.travelportland.com**). *The Oregonian* newspaper also lists special events at **www.oregonlive.com**. To find out what's going on during your visit, pick up a free copy of *Willamette Week* (online at **www.wweek.com**) or buy the Friday or Sunday *Oregonian*. Some of the larger and more popular special and free events are listed there.

Every summer, **Portland Parks and Recreation** (© 503/823-2223) also sponsors a variety of concerts in several parks throughout the city.

February

Portland International Film Festival (© **503/221-1156;** www. nwfilm.org). Though it's not one of the country's top film festivals, it does book plenty of interesting films. Screenings are held at various theaters around the city. Tickets go on sale 2 weeks before the festival starts, and weekend shows usually sell out. Last 3 weeks of February.

May

Cinco de Mayo Fiesta (© **503/222-9807;** www.cincodemayo. org), in downtown Portland at Tom McCall Waterfront Park. This Hispanic celebration with food and entertainment is the largest Cinco de Mayo Fiesta in the country. It's staged in conjunction with Portland's sister city, Guadalajara, Mexico. Early May.

Mother's Day Rhododendron Show (© 503/771-8386 or 503/777-1734; www.arsportland.org), Crystal Springs Rhododendron Gardens. This show comes when the rhododendron blooms are just about at their peak. Mother's Day.

Memorial Day Wine Tastings (© **503/646-2985;** www. yamhillwine.com), throughout the wine country surrounding

Portland. Memorial Day weekend is one of 2 weekends celebrated by Yamhill County and other area wineries with special tastings and events. Many wineries not usually open to the public open on this weekend.

June

Rhythm and Zoo Concerts, Oregon Zoo (© **503/226-1561;** www.oregonzoo.org). Wednesday and Thursday nights from June to August, the zoo's amphitheater hosts performances of folk, jazz, blues, country, and ethnic music with both local and national acts. The ticket price of $8 includes zoo admission.

Zoo Beat Concerts, Oregon Zoo (© **503/226-1561;** www.oregonzoo.org). On selected weekend nights from June to August name performers appear at the zoo. Tickets are $16 to $22.

Portland Rose Festival. From its beginnings back in 1888, when the first rose show was held, the Rose Festival has blossomed into Portland's biggest celebration. The festivities now span nearly a month and include a rose show, parade, rose queen contest, music festival, art show, car races, footrace, boat races, and even an air show. For more details, contact the Portland Rose Festival Association, 5603 SW Hood Ave., Portland, OR 97201 (© **503/227-2681;** www.rosefestival.org), or Ticketmaster (© **503/224-4400**) for tickets to specific events. Tickets are also available through the Rose Festival website. Most of the events (some of which are free) take place during the middle 2 weeks of June, and hotel rooms can be hard to come by, so plan ahead.

Portland Arts Festival (© **503/227-2681;** www.rosefestival.org), South Park Blocks at Portland State University. More than 100 regional artists are juried into this fine art and crafts show ensuring good-quality art-buying opportunities. Music, theater, local wines and microbrews too. Mid-June.

July

Fourth of July Fireworks, Fort Vancouver, Washington (© **360/693-5481**). This is the largest fireworks display west of the Mississippi. They're set off from Vancouver, just across the river, and you can see them from many spots in Portland. For a close-up view, head up to Jantzen Beach, or for an elevated perspective, drive up into the West Hills.

Waterfront Blues Festival, Waterfront Park (© **503/973-3378;** www.waterfrontbluesfest.com). Attracting both national and regional acts, this festival in downtown Portland's Tom McCall

Waterfront Park on the bank of the Willamette River is one of the biggest blues festivals in the country. The festival is a benefit for the Oregon Food Bank, and the suggested daily admission is $5 plus two cans of food. Early July.

High Noon Tunes (© 503/223-1613), Pioneer Courthouse Square. This is a series of free lunchtime concerts featuring everything from classical music to bluegrass to jazz to Japanese taiko drumming. They're held every Wednesday from July through August.

Oregon Brewers Festival (© 503/778-5917; www.oregon brewfest.com), Tom McCall Waterfront Park. America's largest festival of independent craft brewers features lots of local and international microbrews and music. Last weekend in July.

August

Mount Hood Jazz Festival (© 503/219-9833; www.mthood jazz.com), Mount Hood Community College, Gresham (less than 30 min. from Portland). For the serious jazz fan, this is *the* festival of the summer, featuring the greatest names in jazz. Tickets are $28.50 to $50 per day or $70 to $175 for a 3-day pass. Tickets are available through the Web address or Fastixx (© 800/992-8499 or 503/224-8499). First weekend in August.

The Bite—A Taste of Portland (© 503/248-0600), Tom McCall Waterfront Park. Portland's finest restaurants serve up sample portions of their specialties at this food and music festival. It's a true gustatory extravaganza, and also includes wine tasting. This is a benefit for the Special Olympics. Mid-August.

September

Reptile and Amphibian Show, Oregon Museum of Science & Industry (© 503/797-4588). Hundreds of reptiles and amphibians are brought in for a holiday weekend show that's the biggest of its kind in the Northwest. Kids love this venomous event! Labor Day weekend.

Portland Creative Conference, Downtown Portland (© 503/234-1641; www.cre8con.org). Directors, actors, designers, and other creative sorts gather to celebrate and explore the human creative spirit. Past presenters have included local celebs Gus Van Sant and Matt Groening. Mid-September.

Rheinlander Oktoberfest, Oaks Park Amusement Center (© 503/233-5777). A large and crowded Oktoberfest with lots of polka in the beer hall. Late September.

North by Northwest (NXNW), in clubs around the Portland area (② **503/243-2122,** ext. 380, or 512/467-7979; www.nxnw. com). This contemporary music binge features 300 of the hottest regional bands. In addition to the music showcases, there are panels, workshops, and a trade show. Late September.

Portland Marathon, Downtown Portland (② **503/226-1111**). Includes a variety of competitions including a 26.2-mile walk, a 5-mile run, and a kid's run. End of September.

October

Howloween, Oregon Zoo (② 503/226-1561; www.oregonzoo. org). Sort of a trick-or-treat scavenger hunt, with lots of activities for kids. Last weekend in October.

November

Wine Country Thanksgiving, Yamhill County (② 503/ 646-2985; www.yamhillwine.com). About 30 miles outside of Portland, more than two dozen wineries open their doors for tastings of new releases, usually with food and live music. Thanksgiving weekend.

Christmas at Pittock Mansion, Pittock Mansion (② 503/ 823-3623). Each year, this grand French Renaissance–style château is decorated according to an annual theme. Thanksgiving to end of December.

December

Holiday Parade of Ships, Willamette and Columbia rivers (www.christmasships.org). Boats decked out in fanciful holiday lights parade and circle on the rivers after nightfall. Mid-December.

Zoo Lights, Oregon Zoo (② 503/226-1561; www.oregonzoo. org). One of Portland's most impressive holiday light shows is at the Oregon Zoo. No, they don't put lights on the animals, but just about everything else seems to get covered. Month of December (closed Dec 24–25).

4 Top Websites for Portland

CITY GUIDES

CitySearch Portland. http://portland.citysearch.com

Another in CitySearch's excellent line of city sites, CitySearch Portland offers, in a familiar format, much of what a visitor needs to know about the culinary, artistic, theatrical, and musical scenes in town. The site is searchable by time, venue, date, or neighborhood. Also check out the dozens of restaurant reviews, listed by cuisine type.

Visit Portland. www.pova.com

The Portland Oregon Visitors Association (POVA) is eager to have you see and do all you can in its city. Click on "Visitor Information" for advice on sightseeing, performing arts, shopping, outdoor activities, and an online hotel reservation service. The site also offers a calendar of events with special activities highlighted, as well as tools to help business travelers plan meetings and conventions.

Portland, Oregon in 3D. www.pdx3d.com

This one isn't essential, but it's worth visiting for its views of Portland scenes. Use VRML technology to move through Portland's many bridges in 3-D action.

NEWSPAPERS

Oregon Live. www.oregonlive.com

A service of the state's largest newspaper, the *Oregonian,* Oregon Live offers news updates, events calendars, local entertainment listings, online classifieds, and chat rooms.

TOP ATTRACTIONS

The Bridges of Portland. www.bizave.com/portland/bridges

If you're driving in Portland, chances are that you'll be using at least one bridge. For those interested in such things, Andrew Hall has compiled a site detailing the histories and architecture of the city's numerous spans.

Oregon Ballet Theater. www.obt.org

This small, attractive, but infrequently updated site offers a description of each performance during the entire dance season. The page is not particularly deep, but you'll get the necessary information on schedules and ticket ordering.

Oregon Golf. www.oregongolf.com

The grass really is greener in the Pacific Northwest, and this website offers the duffer useful information about courses, both local and statewide. You can also use the handy mileage table to figure out how far you need to go to reach that out-of-town nugget with greens fees for a song.

Oregon Museum of Science and Industry. www.omsi.edu

This is a museum of "everything interesting," and its website certainly represents this. The descriptions of exhibits and events are enough to pique your interest, but OMSI doesn't stop there. Teaming up with the Science Learning Center, the museum offers its own online exhibit, featuring such activities as Water Works (investigate fountains, then create your own), Air Travelers (explore the basic principles of buoyancy), and the ever-vital Rat Cam (a look at the world through the eyes of a museum rat).

Oregon Zoo. www.oregonzoo.org

This is the orca of zoo websites, offering a snappy, well-organized, and extremely thorough layout. Search this site as an animal lover (go to fact sheets about nearly every animal in the zoo, and other zoos as well), or as a potential visitor (not only will they tell you how to get there, they'll tell you how much money to bring).

Portland Art Museum. www.pam.org

Short of an online display of all the artwork, this is everything you could want in a museum site. Here you can take a tour of selected works from the permanent collection, complete with detailed explanations. An extensive list of exhibits will tell you all you need to know about what's showing, and a searchable events calendar keeps you updated.

Portland Center Stage. www.pcs.org

Representing one of the largest theater companies in the country, the PCS site offers a rundown of current and upcoming shows, information on the theater itself, and the chance to purchase tickets online through Ticketmaster.

Portland Opera. www.portlandopera.org

Spartan but informative, this site offers descriptions of current and upcoming productions, and a ticket section that provides seating charts and price lists.

Portland Saturday Market. www.saturdaymarket.org

Get the lowdown on the largest open-air arts-and-crafts market in the United States, including hours of operation, an entertainment calendar, a list of artists, and numerous market facts (it has only closed twice in its history, once for a blizzard and once for a volcanic eruption).

GETTING AROUND

Portland International Airport. www.portlandairportpdx.com

Check out arrivals and departures online—no need to burrow through an automated phone system to see whether your plane is on time. You can also get a complete rundown on parking options and local ground transportation.

Tri-Met (public transportation). www.tri-met.org

Get routes, timetables, and fares, or download the Tri-Met trip planner to find the shortest route between two points via light rail and bus systems.

5 Tips for Travelers with Special Needs

FOR TRAVELERS WITH DISABILITIES

All major hotels listed in this book feature handicapped-accessible rooms, but when making a hotel reservation, be sure to ask. B&Bs, on the other hand, are often in old homes with stairs, and rarely have handicapped-accessible rooms.

All MAX light-rail system stations have wheelchair lifts, and there are two wheelchair spaces available on each train. Be sure to wait on the platform lift. Many of the Tri-Met buses are also equipped with wheelchair lifts and wheelchair spaces. Look for the wheelchair symbol on buses, schedules, and bus stops. There is also a special door-to-door service provided for people who are not able to use the regular Tri-Met service, but as a visitor you must have an eligibility card from another public transportation system. For more information, contact Tri-Met at © **503/962-2455** or 503/802-8200.

Broadway Cab (© **503/227-1234**) and **Radio Cab** (© **503/ 227-1212**) both have vehicles for transporting persons with disabilities.

FOR GAY & LESBIAN TRAVELERS

Gay and lesbian travelers visiting Portland should be sure to pick up a free copy of *Just Out* (© **503/236-1252;** www.justout.com), a bimonthly newspaper for the gay community covering local and national news. You can usually find copies at **Powell's Books,** 1005 W. Burnside St. *Just Out* also publishes the *Just Out Pocketbook,* a statewide gay and lesbian business directory.

Another publication to look for once you're in Portland is *Portland's Gay & Lesbian Community Yellow Pages* (© **503/230-7701;** www.pdxgayyellowpages.com), which is also usually available at Powell's.

FOR SENIORS

Most Portland attractions, many theaters and performance venues, many budget hotels and motels, and Portland's public transportation system all offer senior discounts.

Mention the fact that you're a senior citizen when you first make your travel reservations, since many airlines offer discounts. Both

Amtrak (© **800/USA-RAIL**; www.amtrak.com) and **Greyhound** (© **800/752-4841**; www.greyhound.com) offer discounts to persons over 62. And many hotels offer senior discounts; **Choice Hotels** (Clarion Hotels, Quality Inns, Comfort Inns, Sleep Inns, Econo Lodges, Friendship Inns, and Rodeway Inns), for example, give 30% off their published rates to anyone over 50, provided you book your room through their nationwide toll-free reservations numbers (not directly with the hotels or through a travel agent).

If you aren't a member of the **AARP**, 601 E St. NW, Washington, DC 20049 (© **800/424-3410**; www.aarp.org), you should consider joining. This association provides discounts for many lodgings, car rentals, airfares, and attractions throughout Oregon.

6 Getting There

BY PLANE

Almost 20 carriers serve **Portland Airport** (www.portlandairport pdx.com) from some 100 cities worldwide. The major airlines include **Alaska Airlines** (© 800/426-0333; www.alaskaair.com), **America West** (© 800/235-9292; www.americawest.com), **American Airlines** (© 800/433-7300; www.aa.com), **Continental** (© 800/525-0280; www.continental.com), **Delta** (© 800/221-1212; www.delta.com), **Frontier Airlines** (© 800/432-1359; www.frontierairlines.com), **Hawaiian** (© 800/367-5320; www.hawaiianair.com), **Horizon Air** (© 800/547-9308; www.horizonair.com), **Northwest/KLM** (© 800/225-2525; www.nwa.com), **Skywest** (© 800/241-6522; www.skywest.com), **Southwest** (© 800/435-9792; www.southwest.com), **TWA** (© 800/221-2000; www.twa.com), and **United Airlines** (© 800/241-6522; www.united.com).

FLYING FOR LESS: TIPS FOR GETTING THE BEST AIRFARES

If you happen to be flying from another city on the West Coast or somewhere else in the West, check with Frontier Airlines, Shuttle by United, Alaska Airlines, Horizon Airlines, or Southwest. These airlines often have the best fares between western cities.

Periodically airlines lower prices on their most popular routes. Check your newspaper for advertised discounts or call the airlines directly and ask if any **promotional rates** or special fares are available. You'll almost never see a sale during the peak summer vacation months of July and August, or during the Thanksgiving or Christmas seasons; but in periods of low-volume travel, you should pay no more than $400 for a cross-country flight. If your schedule is flexible, ask if you can secure a cheaper fare by staying an extra day or by flying midweek. (Many airlines won't volunteer this information.) If you already hold a ticket when a sale breaks, it may even pay to exchange your ticket, which usually incurs a $50 to $75 charge.

Note, however, that the lowest-priced fares are often nonrefundable, require advance purchase of 1 to 3 weeks and a certain length of stay, and carry penalties for changing dates of travel.

Consolidators, also known as bucket shops, are a good place to find low fares. Consolidators buy seats in bulk from the airlines and then sell them back to the public at prices below even the airlines' discounted rates. Their small ads usually run in the Sunday travel section at the bottom of the page. Before you pay, however, ask for a confirmation number from the consolidator and then call the airline itself to confirm your seat. Be prepared to book your ticket with a different consolidator—there are many to choose from—if the airline can't confirm your reservation. Also be aware that bucket shop tickets are usually nonrefundable or rigged with stiff cancellation penalties, often as high as 50% to 75% of the ticket price.

Council Travel (℃ **800/226-8624;** www.counciltravel.com) and **STA Travel** (℃ **800/781-4040;** www.statravel.com) cater especially to young travelers, but their bargain basement prices are available to people of all ages. Other reliable consolidators include **1/800-FLY-CHEAP** (www.flycheap.com); and **TFI Tours International** (℃ **800/745-8000** or 212/736-1140), which serves as a clearinghouse for unused seats; or "rebators," such as **Travel Avenue** (℃ **800/333-3335** or 312/876-1116).

BY CAR

Portland is linked to the rest of the United States by a number of interstate highways and smaller roads. I-5 runs north to Seattle and south as far as San Diego. I-84 runs east as far as Salt Lake City. I-405 arcs around the west and south of downtown Portland. I-205 bypasses the city to the east. U.S. 26 runs west to the coast.

Portland is 640 miles from San Francisco, 175 miles from Seattle, 350 miles from Spokane, and 285 miles from Vancouver, B.C.

AAA (℃ **800/222-4357;** www.aaa.com) will supply members with emergency road service if you have car trouble during your trip. You also get maps and detailed Trip-Tiks that give precise directions, including up-to-date information about areas of construction.

See "Getting Around" in chapter 3, "Getting to Know Portland," for details on driving, parking, and car rentals in Portland.

BY TRAIN

Amtrak's (© **800/872-7245;** www.amtrak.com) *Coast Starlight* train connects Portland with Seattle, San Francisco, Los Angeles, and San Diego and stops at historic **Union Station,** 800 NW Sixth Ave. (© **503/273-4866**), about 10 blocks from the heart of downtown Portland. Between Portland and Seattle there are both regular trains and modern European-style Talgo trains, which make the trip in 3½ to 4 hours versus 4½ hours for the regular train. One-way fares on either type of train run $23 to $36. Talgo trains run between Eugene, Oregon, and Vancouver, British Columbia.

Like the airlines, Amtrak offers several discounted fares; although they're not all based on advance purchase, you have more discount options by reserving early. Amtrak's website features a bargain fares service, Rail SALE.

BY BUS

Portland is served by **Greyhound Bus Lines.** The bus station is at 550 NW Sixth Ave. (© **800/231-2222** or 503/243-2357; www.greyhound.com). From Seattle to Portland it's $24 one-way or $42 round-trip, and takes about 3½ to 4½ hours. From San Francisco to Portland it's $29 to $55 one-way or $55 to $105 round-trip (lower prices available with 7-day advance purchase), and takes anywhere from 15 to 21 hours.

7 For International Visitors

ENTRY REQUIREMENTS

Immigration laws are a political issue in the United States these days, and the following requirements may have changed somewhat by the time you plan your trip. Check at any U.S. embassy or consulate for current information and requirements. You can also access the **U.S. State Department**'s Internet site at **www.state.gov**.

VISAS   The U.S. State Department has a **Visa Waiver Pilot Program** allowing citizens of certain countries to enter the United States without a visa for stays of up to 90 days. At press time these included Andorra, Argentina, Australia, Austria, Belgium, Brunei, Denmark, Finland, France, Germany, Iceland, Ireland, Italy, Japan, Liechtenstein, Luxembourg, Monaco, the Netherlands, New Zealand, Norway, San Marino, Slovenia, Spain, Sweden, Switzerland, and the United Kingdom. Citizens of these countries need only a valid passport and a round-trip air or cruise ticket in their possession upon arrival. If they first enter the United States, they may also visit Mexico, Canada, Bermuda, and/or the Caribbean islands and return to the United States without a visa. Further information is available from any U.S. embassy or consulate. Canadian citizens may enter the United States without visas; they need only proof of residence.

Citizens of all other countries must have (1) a valid passport that expires at least 6 months later than the scheduled end of their visit to the United States, and (2) a tourist visa, which may be obtained without charge from any U.S. consulate.

OBTAINING A VISA   To obtain a visa, the traveler must submit a completed application form (either in person or by mail) with a 1½-inch-square photo, and must demonstrate binding ties to a residence abroad. Usually you can obtain a visa at once or within 24 hours, but it may take longer during the summer rush from June through August. If you cannot go in person, contact the nearest U.S. embassy or consulate for directions on applying by mail. Your travel agent or airline office may also be able to provide you with visa applications and instructions. The U.S. consulate or embassy that issues your visa will determine whether you will be issued a multiple- or single-entry visa and any restrictions regarding the length of your stay.

MEDICAL REQUIREMENTS   Unless you're arriving from an area known to be suffering from an epidemic (particularly cholera or yellow fever), inoculations or vaccinations are not required for entry into the United States. If you have a disease that requires treatment with narcotics or syringe-administered medications, carry a valid signed prescription from your physician to allay any suspicions that you may be smuggling narcotics (a serious offense that carries severe penalties in the United States).

For HIV-positive visitors, requirements for entering the United States are somewhat vague and change frequently. For up-to-the-minute information concerning HIV-positive travelers, contact the Centers for Disease Control's **National Center for HIV** (*✆* **404/ 332-4559;** www.hivatis.org) or the **Gay Men's Health Crisis** (*✆* **212/367-1000;** www.gmhc.org).

DRIVER'S LICENSES   Foreign driver's licenses are mostly recognized in the United States, although you may want to get an international driver's license if your home license is not written in English.

CUSTOMS REQUIREMENTS Every visitor over 21 years of age may bring in, free of duty, the following: (1) 1 liter of wine or hard liquor; (2) 200 cigarettes, 100 cigars (but not from Cuba), or 3 pounds of smoking tobacco; and (3) $100 worth of gifts. These exemptions are offered to travelers who spend at least 72 hours in the United States and who have not claimed them within the preceding 6 months. It is altogether forbidden to bring into the country foodstuffs (particularly fruit, cooked meats, and canned goods) and plants (vegetables, seeds, tropical plants, and the like). Foreign tourists may bring in or take out up to $10,000 in U.S. or foreign currency with no formalities; larger sums must be declared to U.S. Customs on entering or leaving, which includes filing form CM 4790. For more specific information regarding U.S. Customs, call your nearest U.S. embassy or consulate, or the **U.S. Customs** office at $\textcircled{C}$ **202/927-1770** (www.customs.ustreas.gov).

MONEY
CURRENCY The U.S. monetary system has a decimal base: one American **dollar** ($1) = 100 **cents** (100¢).

Dollar bills commonly come in $1 (a "buck"), $5, $10, $20, $50, and $100 denominations (the last two are not welcome when paying for small purchases and are not accepted in taxis). There are also $2 bills (seldom encountered). Note that newly redesigned $100 and $50 bills were introduced in 1996, a redesigned $20 bill in 1998 and redesigned $10 and $5 bills in the year 2000. Despite rumors to the contrary, the old-style bills are still legal tender.

There are six denominations of coins: 1¢ (1 cent, or a "penny"), 5¢ (5 cents, or a "nickel"), 10¢ (10 cents, or a "dime"), 25¢ (25 cents, or a "quarter"), 50¢ (50 cents, or a "half dollar"), and, prized by collectors, the rare $1 piece (the older, large silver dollar and the newer, small Susan B. Anthony coin). A new gold-colored $1 piece was introduced in 2000. Note that U.S. coins are not stamped with their numeric value.

The foreign-exchange bureaus so common in Europe are rare even at airports in the United States, and nonexistent outside major cities. Try to avoid having to change foreign money or traveler's checks not denominated in U.S. dollars at a small-town bank, or even a branch bank in a big city. In fact, leave any currency other than U.S. dollars at home—it may prove more nuisance to you than it's worth.

TRAVELER'S CHECKS Traveler's checks *denominated in U.S. dollars* are readily accepted at most hotels, motels, restaurants, and large stores, but may not be accepted at small stores or for small purchases. The best place to change traveler's checks is at a bank. Do not bring traveler's checks denominated in other currencies. The three traveler's checks that are most widely recognized are **Visa, American Express,** and **Thomas Cook.**

CREDIT CARDS & ATMs   Credit cards are the most widely used form of payment in the United States: **Visa** (BarclayCard in Britain), **MasterCard** (EuroCard in Europe, Access in Britain, Chargex in Canada), **American Express, Diners Club,** and **Discover.** You must have a credit or charge card to rent a car. There are, however, a handful of stores and restaurants that do not take credit cards, so be sure to ask in advance. Most businesses display a sticker near their entrance to let you know which cards they accept. (*Note:* Often businesses require a minimum purchase price, usually around $10, to use a credit card.)

It is strongly recommended that you bring at least one major credit card. Hotels, car-rental companies, and airlines usually require a credit-card imprint as a deposit against expenses, and in an emergency, a credit card can be priceless.

You'll find automated-teller machines (ATMs) on just about every block—at least in almost every town—across the country. Some ATMs will allow you to draw U.S. currency against your bank and credit cards. Check with your bank before leaving home, and remember that you will need your personal identification number (PIN) to do so. Most accept Visa, MasterCard, and American Express, as well as ATM cards from other U.S. banks. Expect to be charged up to $3 per transaction, however. One way around these fees is to ask for cash back at grocery stores that accept ATM cards and don't charge usage fees. Of course, you'll have to purchase something first.

3

Getting to Know Portland

1 Orientation

ARRIVING

BY PLANE

Portland International Airport (**PDX**; ✆ **877/739-4636;** www.portlandairportpdx.com) is located 10 miles northeast of downtown Portland, adjacent to the Columbia River. There's an information booth by the baggage-claim area where you can pick up maps and brochures and find out about transportation into the city. Many hotels near the airport provide courtesy shuttle service to and from the airport; be sure to ask when you make a reservation.

GETTING INTO THE CITY BY CAR   If you've rented a car at the airport and want to reach central Portland, follow signs for downtown. These signs will take you first to I-205 and then I-84 west, which brings you to the Willamette River. Take the Morrison Bridge exit to cross the river. The trip takes about 20 minutes and is entirely on interstates. For more information on renting a car, see section 2 of this chapter, "Getting Around," below.

GETTING INTO THE CITY BY TAXI, SHUTTLE, BUS, OR LIGHT RAIL   If you haven't rented a car at the airport, the best way to get into town is to take the new **Airport MAX (Red Line)** light-rail system, which at press time, was scheduled to go into service in September 2001. This light-rail line will operate daily every 15 minutes between 5am and 11:30pm and the trip from the airport to Pioneer Courthouse Square in downtown Portland will take approximately 40 minutes. (All but one or two of the downtown hotels lie within 4 or 5 blocks of the square; plan on walking since there are not usually any taxis waiting here. Folks arriving with a lot of luggage will be better off taking a cab or shuttle van from the airport.) The fare is $1.55. For information on this new service, contact **Tri-Met** (✆ **503/238-7433;** www.tri-met.org).

Alternatively, you can take the **Gray Line Airport Shuttle** (✆ **800/422-7042** or 503/285-9845), which picks you up outside

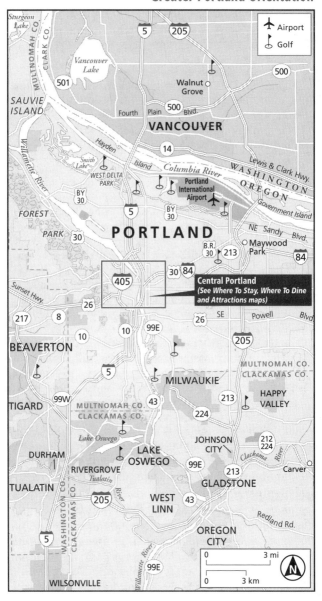

the baggage-claim area and can drop you at any of 16 downtown hotels. One-way fares are $15 for adults, $12 seniors, $8 for children 4 to 12, and free for children under 4. It operates every 45 minutes from 5:15am to midnight.

Tri-Met public bus no. 12 leaves the airport approximately every 15 minutes from 5:30am to 11:45pm for the trip to downtown Portland. The trip takes about 40 minutes and costs $1.25. The bus between downtown and the airport operates between 5:15am and 12:30am and leaves from SW Sixth Avenue and Main Street.

A taxi downtown generally costs between $20 and $25 and is cheaper and faster than the Gray Line Airport Shuttle if there are two or more of you traveling together.

BY TRAIN/BUS

Amtrak trains stop at the historic **Union Station,** 800 NW Sixth Ave. (© **503/273-4866**), about 10 blocks from the heart of downtown Portland. Taxis are usually waiting to meet trains and can take you to your hotel. Alternatively, you might be able to get your hotel to send a van to pick you up, or, if you are renting a car from a downtown car-rental office, the agency will usually pick you up at the station. Public buses stop within a block of the station and are free within the downtown area if you catch the bus south of Hoyt Street (2 blocks away).

The **Greyhound Bus Lines** station is at 550 NW Sixth Ave. (© **800/231-2222** or 503/243-2357) on the north side of downtown near Union Station. As with getting into downtown from the train station, if you walk south 2 blocks to Hoyt Street, you reach the edge of downtown Portland's Fareless Square area, within which all buses and light-rail trolleys are free.

Although you could easily walk from the station into the heart of downtown, you have to pass through a somewhat rough neighborhood for a few blocks. This area is currently undergoing a renaissance and is not nearly as bad as it once was.

VISITOR INFORMATION

The **Portland Oregon Visitors Association (POVA) Information Center,** 701 SW Sixth Ave., Suite 1 (© **877/678-5263** or 503/ 275-9750; www.travelportland.com), is in Pioneer Courthouse Square in downtown Portland. There's also an information booth by the baggage-claim area at the Portland Airport.

If you happen to see a person walking down a Portland street wearing a very bright green jacket, he or she is probably a member of the **Portland Guides** service run by the Association for Portland Progress (② **503/224-7383**). The guides will be happy to answer any question you have about the city.

CITY LAYOUT

Portland is in northwestern Oregon at the confluence of the Columbia and Willamette Rivers. To the west are the West Hills, which rise to more than 1,000 feet. Some 90 miles west of the West Hills are the spectacular Oregon coast and the Pacific Ocean. To the east are rolling hills that extend to the Cascade Range, about 50 miles away. The most prominent peak in this section of the Cascades is Mount Hood (11,235 ft.), a dormant volcanic peak that looms over the city on clear days. From many parts of Portland it's also possible to see Mount St. Helens, the volcano that famously erupted in 1980.

With about 1.8 million people in the entire metropolitan area, Portland remains a relatively small city. This is especially evident when you begin to explore the compact downtown area. Nearly everything is accessible on foot, and the city authorities do everything they can to encourage walking.

MAIN ARTERIES & STREETS   I-84 (Banfield Fwy. or Expressway) enters Portland from the east. East of the city is **I-205,** which bypasses downtown Portland and runs past the airport. **I-5 (East Bank Fwy.)** runs through on a north-south axis, passing along the east bank of the Willamette River directly across from downtown. **I-405 (Stadium Fwy. and Foothills Fwy.)** circles around the west and south sides of downtown. **U.S. 26 (Sunset Hwy.)** leaves downtown heading west toward Beaverton and the coast. **Oregon Highway 217 (Beaverton-Tigard Hwy.)** runs south from U.S. 26 in Beaverton.

The most important artery within Portland is **Burnside Street.** This is the dividing line between north and south Portland. Dividing the city from east to west is the **Willamette River,** which is crossed by eight bridges in the downtown area. From north to south these bridges are the Fremont, Broadway, Steel, Burnside, Morrison, Hawthorne, Marquam, and Ross Island. Additional bridges beyond the downtown area include the Sellwood Bridge between downtown and Lake Oswego and the St. John's Bridge from northwest Portland to north Portland.

For the sake of convenience, we have defined downtown Portland as the 300-block area within the **Fareless Square.** This is the area (shaded in on the map on p. 25) in which you can ride for free on the city's public buses and the MAX light-rail system. In downtown, the Fareless Square is bounded by I-405 on the west and south, by Hoyt Street on the north, and by the Willamette River on the east. A Fareless Square extension now allows transit riders to travel between downtown Portland and both the Oregon Convention Center and Lloyd Center Mall for free. There is no charge to ride either the MAX light-rail trolleys or any of the 10 buses that connect downtown with the Rose Quarter and Lloyd District across the Willamette River in northeast Portland.

FINDING AN ADDRESS   Finding an address in Portland can be easy. Almost all addresses in Portland, and for miles beyond, include a map quadrant—NE (Northeast), SW (Southwest), and so forth. The dividing line between east and west is the Willamette River; between north and south it's Burnside Street. Any downtown address will be labeled either SW (Southwest) or NW (northwest). An exception to this rule is the area known as North Portland, which is the area across the Willamette River from downtown going toward Jantzen Beach. Streets here have a plain "North" designation. Also, Burnside Street is designated either "East" or "West."

Avenues run north–south and streets run east–west. Street names are the same on both sides of the Willamette River. Consequently,

---

Fun Fact Did You Know?

- The flasher in the famous "Expose Yourself to Art" poster is none other than Bud Clark, the former mayor of Portland.
- Portland is the only city in the United States with an extinct volcano—Mount Tabor—within the city limits.
- Matt Groening, creator of *The Simpsons,* got his start in Portland.
- More Asian elephants have been born in Portland (at the Metro Washington Park Zoo) than in any other city in North America.
- Twenty downtown water fountains were a gift to the city from teetotaling early-20th-century timber baron Simon Benson, who wanted his mill workers to have something other than alcohol to drink during the day.

there is a Southwest Yamhill Street and a Southeast Yamhill Street. In northwest Portland, street names are alphabetical going north from Burnside to Wilson. Naito Parkway is the street nearest the Willamette River on the west side, and Water Avenue is the nearest on the east side. Beyond these are numbered avenues. On the west side you'll also find Broadway and Park Avenue between Sixth Avenue and Ninth Avenue. With each block, the addresses increase by 100, beginning at the Willamette River for avenues and at Burnside Street for streets. Odd numbers are generally on the west and north sides of the street, and even numbers on the east and south sides.

Here's an example: You want to go to 1327 SW Ninth Ave. Because it's in the 1300 block, you'll find it 13 blocks south of Burnside and, because it's an odd number, on the west side of the street.

STREET MAPS Stop by the **Portland Oregon Visitors Association Information Center,** 701 SW Sixth Ave., Suite 1 (© **877/678-5263** or 503/275-9750; www.travelportland.com), in Pioneer Courthouse Square in downtown Portland for a free map of the city; they also have a more detailed one for sale.

Powell's City of Books, 1005 W. Burnside St. (© **800/878-7323** or 503/228-4651), has an excellent free map of downtown that includes a walking-tour route and information on many of the sights you'll pass along the way.

Members of the **American Automobile Association (AAA)** can get a free map of the city at the AAA offices at 600 SW Market St. (© **503/222-6734;** www.aaa.com).

PORTLAND NEIGHBORHOODS IN BRIEF

Portland's neighborhoods are mostly dictated by geography. The Willamette River forms a natural dividing line between the eastern and western portions of the city, while the Columbia River forms a boundary with the state of Washington on the north. The West Hills, comprising Portland's prime residential neighborhoods, are a beautiful backdrop for this attractive city. Covered in evergreens, the hills rise to a height of 1,000 feet at the edge of downtown. Within these hills are the Oregon Zoo, the International Rose Test Garden, the Japanese Garden, and several other attractions.

For a map of Portland neighborhoods, turn to the "Portland Attractions" map on p. 82–83.

DOWNTOWN This term usually refers to the business and shopping district south of Burnside and north of Jackson Street between the Willamette River and 13th Avenue. Here you'll find a dozen or more high-end hotels, dozens of restaurants of all types, and loads of shopping (including the major department stores). Within downtown's **Cultural District** (along Broadway and the South Park Blocks), are most of the city's performing arts venues and a couple of museums.

SKIDMORE HISTORIC DISTRICT   Also known as Old Town, this is Portland's original commercial core and centers around Southwest Ankeny Street and Southwest First Avenue. Many of the restored buildings have become retail stores, but despite the presence of the **Saturday Market,** the neighborhood has never become a popular shopping district, mostly because of its welfare hotels, missions, street people, and drug dealing. However, with its many clubs and bars, it has become the city's main nightlife district. The neighborhood is safe during the day, but solo women should exercise caution at night.

CHINATOWN   Portland has had a Chinatown almost since its earliest days. This small area, with its numerous Chinese groceries and restaurants, is wedged between the Pearl District and the Skidmore Historic District and is entered through the colorful Chinatown Gate at West Burnside Street and Fourth Avenue. The neighborhood's main attraction is the impressive **Portland Classical Chinese Garden.** Because of its proximity to bars on West Burnside Street and the homeless missions and welfare hotels in Old Town, this is not a good neighborhood to explore late at night.

THE PEARL DISTRICT   This neighborhood of galleries, residential and business lofts, cafes, breweries, and shops is bounded by the North Park Blocks, Lovejoy Street, I-405, and Burnside Street. Crowds of people come here on **First Thursday** (the first Thurs of every month) when the galleries and other businesses are open late. This is currently Portland's bid for a hip urban loft scene and is one of the city's main upscale restaurant neighborhoods.

NORTHWEST/NOB HILL   Located along Northwest 23rd and Northwest 21st avenues, this is Portland's most fashionable neighborhood. Here you'll find many of the city's most talked-about restaurants (mostly along NW 21st Ave.), as well as lots of cafes, boutiques, and increasingly, national chain stores. Surrounding the two main business streets of the neighborhood are blocks of restored Victorian homes on shady tree-lined streets. This is where you'll find the city's liveliest street scene.

IRVINGTON   Though neither as attractive nor as large as the Northwest/Nob Hill neighborhood, Irvington, centered on

Broadway in northeast Portland, is almost as hip. For several blocks along Broadway (around NE 15th Ave.) you'll find interesting boutiques and numerous excellent but inexpensive restaurants.

HAWTHORNE/BELMONT DISTRICT This enclave of southeast Portland is full of eclectic boutiques, moderately priced restaurants, and hip college students from nearby **Reed College.** Just south of Hawthorne Boulevard, beginning at SE 12th Avenue, you'll find the interesting **Ladd's Addition** neighborhood, which has five rose gardens, a great pastry shop, and a brewpub that features live music several nights a week. Along Belmont Street, just north of Hawthorne Boulevard, is one of the city's up-and-coming hip neighborhoods.

SELLWOOD/WESTMORELAND Situated in Southeast Portland, this is the city's antiques district and contains many restored Victorian houses. Just north of the Sellwood antiques district, surrounding the intersection of SE Milwaukie Avenue and SE Bybee Boulevard, you'll find the heart of the Eastmoreland neighborhood, home to numerous good restaurants.

2 Getting Around

BY PUBLIC TRANSPORTATION

FREE RIDES Portland is committed to keeping its downtown uncongested, and to this end has invested heavily in its public transportation system. The single greatest innovation and best reason to ride the Tri-Met public buses and the MAX light-rail system is that they're free within an area known as the **Fareless Square.** That's right, free!

There are 300 blocks of downtown included in the Fareless Square, and as long as you stay within the boundaries, you don't pay a cent. The Fareless Square covers the area between I-405 on the south and west, Hoyt Street on the north, and the Willamette River on the east. A Fareless Square extension now also makes it possible to take public transit (either the bus or the MAX light-rail trolley) between downtown Portland and both the Rose Quarter (site of the Oregon Convention Center) and the Lloyd District (site of the Lloyd Center Mall), which are both across the Willamette River in northeast Portland.

BY BUS Tri-Met buses operate daily over an extensive network. You can pick up the *Tri-Met Guide,* which lists all the bus routes with times, or individual route maps and time schedules, at the **Tri-Met Customer Assistance Office,** behind and beneath the waterfall fountain at Pioneer Courthouse Square (© **503/238-7433;** www.tri-met.org). The office is open Monday through Friday from 7:30am to 5:30pm. Bus and MAX passes and transit information are also available at area Fred Meyer, Safeway, and most Albertson grocery stores. Nearly all Tri-Met buses pass through the Transit Mall on SW Fifth Avenue and SW Sixth Avenue.

Outside the Fareless Square, adult fares on both Tri-Met buses and MAX are $1.25 or $1.55, depending on how far you travel. Seniors 65 years and older pay 60¢ with valid proof of age; children 7 through 18 pay 95¢. You can also make free transfers between the bus and the MAX light-rail system. A day ticket costing $4 is good for travel to all zones and is valid on both buses and MAX. Day tickets can be purchased from any bus driver. The **Adventure Pass,** good for 3 days of unlimited rides on both buses and MAX, costs $10 and is available at the Tri-Met Customer Assistance Office and at any of the other outlets mentioned above.

BY LIGHT RAIL   The Metropolitan Area Express (MAX) is Portland's aboveground light-rail system that connects downtown Portland with the airport (as of Sept 2001), the eastern suburb of Gresham, and the western suburbs of Beaverton and Hillsboro. MAX is basically a modern trolley, but there are also reproductions of vintage trolley cars (© **503/323-7363**) operating between downtown Portland and the Lloyd Center on Sundays between noon and 6pm. One of the most convenient places to catch the MAX is at Pioneer Courthouse Square. The MAX light-rail system crosses the Transit Mall on SW Morrison Street and SW Yamhill Street. Transfers to the bus are free.

As with the bus, MAX is free within the Fareless Square, which includes all the downtown area. A Fareless Square extension now also makes it possible to ride the MAX between downtown Portland and both the Rose Quarter (site of the Oregon Convention Center) and the Lloyd District (site of the Lloyd Center Mall). Both are across the Willamette River in northeast Portland. If you are traveling outside of the Fareless Square, be sure to buy your ticket and stamp it in the time-punch machine on the platform before you board MAX. There are ticket-vending machines at all MAX stops that tell you how much to pay for your destination; these machines also give change. The MAX driver cannot sell tickets. Fares are the same as on buses. There are ticket inspectors who randomly check to make sure passengers have stamped tickets.

In July 2001, the new **Portland Streetcar** (© **503/238-RIDE;** www.portlandstreetcar.org) began operating between the Portland State University neighborhood of downtown through the Pearl District to the Nob Hill neighborhood. The route takes in not only the attractions of the Cultural District, but also all the restaurants and great shopping in the Pearl District and along Northwest 21st and 23rd avenues, which makes this streetcar a great way for visitors to get from the downtown (where most of the hotels are located) to the neighborhoods with the greatest concentrations of restaurants. On Saturdays and Sundays, vintage streetcars operate free of charge (donations are encouraged). Streetcar fares for trips outside the Fareless Square are $1.25 for adults, 95¢ for youths, and 60¢ for seniors.

BY CAR

CAR RENTALS   Portland is a compact city, and public transit will get you to most attractions within its limits. However, if you are planning to explore outside the city—and Portland's greatest attractions, such as Mount Hood and the Columbia River Gorge, lie not in the city itself but in the countryside within an hour of the city—you'll definitely need a car.

The major car-rental companies are all represented in Portland and have desks at Portland International Airport, which is the most convenient place to pick up a car. There are also many independent and smaller car-rental agencies listed in the Portland Yellow Pages. Currently, weekly rates for an economy car in July (high-season rates) are about $188 with no discounts. Expect lower rates in the rainy months.

On the ground floor of the airport parking deck, across the street from the baggage-claim area, you'll find the following companies: **Avis** (© 800/831-2847 or 503/249-4950; www.avis.com), **Budget** (© 800/527-0700 or 503/249-6500; www.budget.com), **Dollar** (© 800/800-4000 or 503/249-4792; www.dollar.com), **Hertz** (© 800/654-3131 or 503/249-8216; www.hertz.com), and **National** (© 800/227-7368 or 503/249-4900; www.nationalcar.com). Outside the airport, but with desks adjacent to the other car-rental desks, are **Alamo** (© 800/327-9633 or 503/252-7039; www.alamo.com), **Enterprise** (© 800/736-8222 or 503/252-1500; www.enterprise. com), and **Thrifty,** at 10800 NE Holman St. (© 800/367-2277 or 503/254-6563; www.thrifty.com).

PARKING   Parking downtown can be a problem, especially if you show up after workers have gotten to their offices on weekdays. There are a couple of very important things to remember when parking downtown. When parking on the street, be sure to notice the meter's time limit. These vary from as little as 15 minutes (these are always located right in front of the restaurant or museum where you plan to spend 2 hr.) to long term (read: long walk). Most common are 30- and 60-minute meters. You don't have to feed the meters after 6pm or on Sunday.

The best parking deal in town is at the **Smart Park** garages, where the cost is 95¢ per hour for the first 4 hours (but after that the hourly rate jumps considerably and you'd be well advised to move your car), $2 for the entire evening after 6pm, or $5 all day on the weekends. Look for the red, white, and black signs featuring Les Park, the friendly parking attendant. You'll find Smart Park garages at First Avenue and Jefferson Street, Fourth Avenue and Yamhill Street, Tenth Avenue and Yamhill Street, Third Avenue and Alder Street, O'Bryant Square, and Naito Parkway and Davis Street. More than 200 downtown merchants also validate Smart Park tickets if you spend at least $25, so don't forget to take your ticket along with you.

Rates in other public lots range from about $1.50 up to about $4 per hour.

SPECIAL DRIVING RULES   You may turn right on a red light after a full stop, and if you are in the far left lane of a one-way street, you may turn left into the adjacent left lane of a one-way street at a red light after a full stop. Everyone in a moving vehicle is required to wear a seat belt.

BY TAXI

Because most everything in Portland is fairly close, getting around by taxi can be economical. Although there are almost always taxis waiting in line at major hotels, you won't find them cruising the streets—you'll have to phone for one. **Broadway Cab** (② 503/227-1234) and **Radio Cab** (② 503/227-1212) both offer 24-hour radio-dispatched service and accept American Express, Discover, MasterCard, and Visa. Fares are $2.50 for the first mile, $1.50 for each additional mile, and $1 for additional passengers. Up to four passengers can share a taxi.

ON FOOT

City blocks in Portland are about half the size of most city blocks elsewhere, and the entire downtown area covers only about 13 blocks by 26 blocks. This makes Portland a very easy place to explore on foot. The city has been very active in encouraging people to get out of their cars and onto the sidewalks downtown. The sidewalks are wide and there are many fountains, works of art, and small parks with benches.

As mentioned earlier in this chapter, if you happen to spot a person walking around downtown wearing a bright green jacket, he or she is probably a **Portland Guide.** These informative souls are there to answer any questions you might have about Portland.

 FAST FACTS: Portland

AAA The **American Automobile Association** (℅ 800/222-4357; www.aaa.com) has a Portland office at 600 SW Market St. (℅ **503/222-6734**), which offers free city maps to members.

Airport See "Getting There" in chapter 2 and "Arriving," in section 1 of this chapter.

American Express The **American Express Travel Service Office,** 1100 SW Sixth Ave. (℅ **503/226-2961**), at the corner of Sixth and Main, is open Monday through Friday from 8:30am to 5:30pm. You can cash American Express traveler's checks and exchange the major foreign currencies here. For card member services, phone ℅ **800/528-4800.** Call ℅ **800/AXP-TRIP** or go online to **www.americanexpress.com** for other city locations or general information.

Area Codes The Portland metro area has two area codes—503 and 971—and it is necessary to dial all 10 digits of a telephone number, even when making local calls.

Babysitters If your hotel doesn't offer babysitting services, call **Northwest Nannies** (℅ **503/245-5288**).

Car Rentals See section 2, "Getting Around," earlier in this chapter.

Climate See section 4, "When to Go," in chapter 2.

Dentist Contact **Oregon Dental Referral** (℅ **800/800-1705**) or the **Multnomah Dental Society** (℅ **503/223-4731**) for a referral.

Doctor If you need a physician referral while in Portland, contact the **Medical Society of Metropolitan Portland** (℅ **503/222-0156**). The **Oregon Health Sciences University Hospital,**

3181 SW Sam Jackson Park Rd. ((✆ **503/494-8311**) has a drop-in clinic.

Emergencies For police, fire, or medical emergencies, phone ✆ **911.**

Eyeglass Repair Check out **Binyon's Eyeworld Downtown,** 803 SW Morrison St. (✆ **503/226-6688**).

Hospitals Three conveniently located area hospitals are **Legacy Good Samaritan,** 1015 NW 22nd Ave. (✆ **503/413-7711**); **Providence Portland Medical Center,** 4805 NE Glisan St. (✆ **503/215-1111**); and the **Oregon Health Sciences University Hospital,** 3181 SW Sam Jackson Park Rd. (✆ **503/494-8311**), which is just southwest of the city center and has a drop-in clinic.

Hot Lines The **Portland Center for the Performing Arts Event Information Line** is ✆ **503/796-9293.** The **Oregonian's Inside Line** (✆ **503/225-5555**), operated by Portland's daily newspaper, provides information on everything from concerts and festivals to sports and the weather.

Information See "Visitor Information" in section 1 of this chapter.

Internet Access If you need to check e-mail while you're in Portland, first check with your hotel. Otherwise, visit a **Kinko's.** There's one downtown at 221 SW Alder St. (✆ **503/224-6550**) and in Northwest at 950 NW 23rd Ave. ✆ **503/222-4133**). You can also try the **Multnomah County Library,** 801 SW 10th Ave. (✆ **503/988-5123**), which is Portland's main library and offers online services.

Liquor Laws The legal minimum drinking age in Oregon is 21. Aside from on-premise sales of cocktails in bars and restaurants, hard liquor can only be purchased in liquor stores. Beer and wine are available in convenience stores and grocery stores. Brewpubs tend to sell only beer and wine, but some also have licenses to sell hard liquor.

Maps See "City Layout," in section 1 of this chapter.

Newspapers/Magazines Portland's morning daily newspaper is *The Oregonian.* For arts and entertainment information and listings, consult the "A&E" section of the Friday *Oregonian* or pick up a free copy of *Willamette Week* at Powell's Books and other bookstores, convenience stores, or cafes.

Pharmacies Convenient to most downtown hotels, **Central Drug,** 538 SW Fourth Ave. (© **503/226-2222**), is open Monday through Friday from 9am to 6pm, Saturday from 10am to 4pm.

Photographic Needs **Wolfcamera,** 900 SW Fourth Ave. (© **503/224-6776**) and 733 SW Alder (© **503/224-6775**), offers 1-hour film processing. **Camera World,** 400 SW Sixth Ave. (© **503/205-5900**), is the largest camera and video store in the city.

Police To reach the police, call © **911.**

Post Offices The **main post office,** 715 NW Hoyt St., is open Monday through Friday from 7am to 6:30pm, Saturday from 8:30am to 5pm. There is also another convenient post office at 1505 SW Sixth Ave., open Monday through Friday from 7am to 6pm, Saturday from 10am to 3pm. For more information, call © **800/275-8777.**

Restrooms There are public restrooms underneath Starbucks coffee shop in Pioneer Courthouse Square, in downtown shopping malls, and in hotel lobbies.

Safety Because of its small size and progressive emphasis on keeping the downtown alive and growing, Portland is still a relatively safe city; in fact, strolling the downtown streets at night is a popular pastime. Take extra precautions, however, if you venture into the entertainment district along West Burnside Street or Chinatown at night. Certain neighborhoods in north and northeast Portland are the centers for much of the city's gang activity, so before visiting any place in this area, be sure to get very detailed directions so you don't get lost. If you plan to go hiking in Forest Park, don't leave anything valuable in your car. This holds true in the Skidmore Historic District (Old Town) as well.

Smoking Although many of the restaurants listed in this book are smoke-free, there are also many Portland restaurants that allow smoking. At most high-end restaurants, the smoking area is usually in the bar/lounge, and although many restaurants have separate bar menus, most will serve you off the regular menu even if you are eating in the bar. There are very few nonsmoking bars in Portland.

Taxes Portland is a shopper's paradise—there's no sales tax. However, there is an 11.5% tax on hotel rooms within the city and a 12.5% tax on car rentals (plus an additional airport-use fee if you pick up your rental car at the airport; this fee is usually an additional 11%). Outside the city, the room tax varies.

Taxis See section 2, "Getting Around," earlier in this chapter.

Time Zone Portland is on Pacific time, 3 hours behind the East Coast. In the summer, daylight saving time is observed and clocks are set forward 1 hour.

Transit Info For bus and MAX information, call the **Tri-Met Customer Assistance Office** (ⓒ **503/238-7433**).

Weather If it's summer, it's sunny; otherwise, there's a chance of rain. This almost always suffices, but for specifics, call **Weatherline Forecast Service** (ⓒ **503/243-7575**) or the Portland Oregon Visitor Association's **weather information hot line** (ⓒ **503/275-9792**). If you want to know how to pack before you arrive, check **www.cnn.com/weather** or **www. weather.com**.

4

Where to Stay

Portland has been undergoing a downtown hotel renaissance for the past decade. Several historic hotels have been renovated, and other historic buildings have been retrofitted to serve as hotels. The Benson, the Governor Hotel, The Heathman Hotel, the Hotel Vintage Plaza, the 5th Avenue Suites, and the Embassy Suites (formerly the Multnomah Hotel) are all part of this trend. These hotels offer some of Portland's most comfortable and memorable accommodations. Several other new hotels have also opened in the past 2 years.

The city's largest concentrations of hotels are in downtown and near the airport. If you don't mind the high prices, downtown hotels are the most convenient for visitors.

However, if your budget won't allow for a first-class business hotel, try near the airport or elsewhere on the outskirts of the city (Troutdale and Gresham on the east side; Beaverton and Hillsboro on the west; Wilsonville and Lake Oswego in the south; and Vancouver, Washington, in the north), where you're more likely to find inexpensive to moderately priced motels.

You'll find the greatest concentration of bed-and-breakfasts in the Irvington neighborhood of northeast Portland. This area is close to downtown and is generally quite convenient even if you are here on business.

In the following listings, price categories are based on the rate for a double room in high season. (Most hotels charge the same for a single or double room.) Keep in mind that the rates listed do not include local room taxes, which vary between 7% and 11.5%.

For comparison purposes, we list what hotels call "rack rates," or walk-in rates—but you should never have to pay these highly inflated prices. Various discounts (AAA, senior, corporate, and Entertainment Book) often reduce these rates, so be sure to ask (and check each hotel's website for Internet specials). In fact, you can often get a discounted corporate rate simply by flashing a business card (your own, that is). At inexpensive chain motels, there are almost always discounted rates for AAA members and seniors.

Where to Stay in Portland

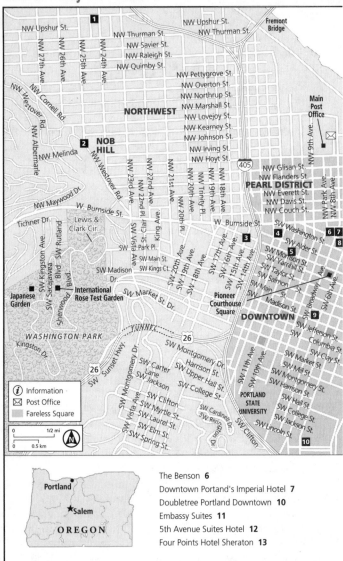

The Benson **6**

Downtown Portland's Imperial Hotel **7**

Doubletree Portland Downtown **10**

Embassy Suites **11**

5th Avenue Suites Hotel **12**

Four Points Hotel Sheraton **13**

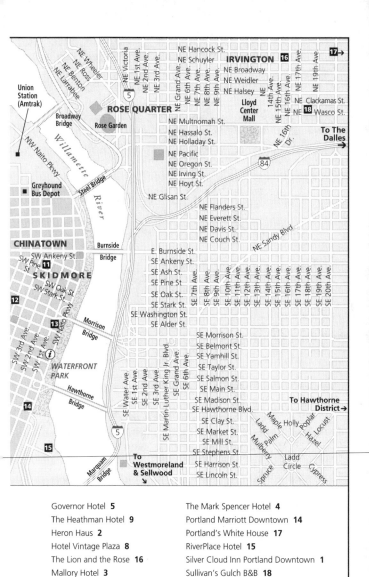

Governor Hotel **5**

The Heathman Hotel **9**

Heron Haus **2**

Hotel Vintage Plaza **8**

The Lion and the Rose **16**

Mallory Hotel **3**

The Mark Spencer Hotel **4**

Portland Marriott Downtown **14**

Portland's White House **17**

RiverPlace Hotel **15**

Silver Cloud Inn Portland Downtown **1**

Sullivan's Gulch B&B **18**

You'll also find that room rates are almost always considerably lower October through April (the rainy season), and large downtown hotels often offer weekend discounts of up to 50% throughout the year. Some of the large, upscale hotel chains have now gone to an airline-type rate system based on occupancy, so if you call early enough before a hotel books up you might get a really good rate. On the other hand, call at the last minute and you might catch a cancellation and still be offered a low rate. Also be sure to ask about special packages (romance, golf, or theater), which most of the more expensive hotels usually offer.

A few hotels include breakfast in their rates; others offer complimentary breakfast only on certain deluxe floors. Parking rates are per day.

Although Portland is not nearly as popular with tourists as Seattle, it's still advisable to make reservations as far in advance as possible if you're planning to visit during the busy summer months.

Most hotels offer nonsmoking rooms, and most bed-and-breakfasts are exclusively nonsmoking. Most hotels also offer wheelchair-accessible rooms.

HELPING HANDS

If you're having trouble booking a room, try the **Portland Oregon Visitors Association (POVA),** 1000 SW Broadway, Suite 2300, Portland, OR 97205 (© 877/678-5263 or 503/275-9750; www.pova.com), which offers a reservation service for the Portland metro area.

For information on **bed-and-breakfasts** in the Portland area, call the **Portland Oregon Visitors Association** (© 877/678-5263 or 503/275-9750; www.pova.com). Also try contacting the **Oregon Bed and Breakfast Guild,** P.O. Box 3187, Ashland, OR 97520 (© **800/944-6196;** www.obbg.org). You can also try the **Northwest Bed and Breakfast Reservation Service** (© 877/243-7782 or 503/243-7616; www.nwbedandbreakfast.com).

1 Downtown

VERY EXPENSIVE

RiverPlace Hotel 𝒜𝒜𝒜   With the Willamette River at its back doorstep and the sloping lawns of Waterfront Park to one side, the RiverPlace is Portland's only downtown waterfront hotel. This alone would be enough to recommend the hotel, but its quiet boutique-hotel atmosphere would make it an excellent choice even if it weren't on the water.

The river-view standard king rooms here are the hotel's best deal, but the junior suites are only slightly more expensive and provide a bit more space. In general, furnishings are neither as elegant nor as luxurious as at The Heathman or The Benson; what you're paying for is the waterfront locale. More than half the rooms are suites; some come with wood-burning fireplaces and whirlpool baths. There are also condominiums for long stays.

The hotel's restaurant overlooks the river, and there's also a comfortable bar with live piano music and a casual menu. The bar also has a patio dining area overlooking the river.

1510 SW Harbor Way, Portland, OR 97201. © **800/227-1333** or 503/228-3233. Fax 503/295-6161. www.riverplacehotel.com. 84 units. $219–$379 double; $249–$389 junior suite; $279–$979 suite. Rates include continental breakfast. AE, DC, DISC, MC, V. Valet parking $18. Pets accepted with $45 nonrefundable cleaning fee. **Amenities:** Restaurant (Northwest/Continental), lounge; indoor pool; access to nearby health club; day spa; Jacuzzi; sauna; concierge; 24-hr. room service; massage; babysitting; laundry/dry cleaning. *In room:* A/C, TV, fax, dataport, minibar, hair dryer, iron.

EXPENSIVE

The Benson ✹✹✹   Built in 1912, The Benson exudes old-world sophistication and elegance. In the French baroque lobby, walnut paneling frames a marble fireplace, Austrian crystal chandeliers hang from the ornate plasterwork ceiling, and a marble staircase allows for grand entrances. Presidents stay here whenever they're in town—a good clue that these are the poshest digs in Portland. The guest rooms vary considerably in size, but all are luxuriously furnished in a plush Euro-luxe styling. The deluxe kings are particularly roomy, but the corner junior suites are the hotel's best deal. Not only are these quite large, but the abundance of windows also makes them much cheerier than other rooms. Bathrooms, unfortunately, have little shelf space.

In the vaults below the lobby you'll find the **London Grill,** well known for its Sunday brunch. Just off the lobby, there's El Gaucho steakhouse, and in the Lobby Bar, there's live jazz in the evenings.

309 SW Broadway, Portland, OR 97205. © **800/426-0670** or 503/228-2000. Fax 503/226-4603. www.bensonhotel.com. 287 units. $150–$170 double; $285 junior suite; $500–$900 suite. AE, DC, DISC, MC, V. Valet parking $21. Pets accepted with $100 fee. **Amenities:** Restaurant (Northwest/Continental), lounge; exercise room, access to nearby health club; concierge; business center; 24-hr. room service; massage; dry cleaning. *In room:* A/C, TV, dataport, minibar, coffeemaker, hair dryer, iron.

Embassy Suites ✹✹ *(Kids) (Value)*   Located in the restored former Multnomah Hotel, which originally opened in 1912, the Embassy

Suites has a beautiful large lobby that is a masterpiece of gilded plasterwork. The accommodations here are primarily two-room suites,
with the exception of a handful of studio suites. In keeping with the
historic nature of the hotel, the suites have classically styled furnishings. However, what's much more important is that they give you
lots of room to spread out, a rarity in downtown hotels. The hotel's
Portland Steak and Chophouse has a classic dark and woody steakhouse decor and a large bar. There's a nightly complimentary
evening manager's reception.

319 SW Pine St., Portland, OR 97204-2726. ✆ **800/EMBASSY** or 503/279-9000.
Fax 503/497-9051. www.embassyportland.com. 276 units. $129–$209 double.
Rates include full breakfast. AE, DC, DISC, MC, V. Valet parking $15; self-parking
$15. **Amenities:** Restaurant (steak), lounge; indoor pool; exercise room, access to
nearby health club; day spa; Jacuzzi; sauna; concierge; car-rental desk; business
center; room service; massage; laundry/dry cleaning. *In room:* A/C, TV, dataport,
fridge, coffeemaker, hair dryer, iron.

5th Avenue Suites Hotel 𝒜𝒜   Located a block from Pioneer
Courthouse Square and within a few blocks of the best downtown
shopping, this unpretentious yet sophisticated hotel is housed in
what was originally a department store. Artwork by Northwest
artists fills the lobby, and in the afternoon there are complimentary
tastings of Oregon and Washington wines.

Guest rooms, most of which are suites, are furnished in a turn-of-
the-century country style but also have fax machines and two-line
speakerphones for 21st-century convenience. Plush chairs and beds
with padded headboards and luxurious comforters assure that business travelers (and others) will be comfortable in their home away
from office. Bathrooms have lots of counter space. In the suites,
sliding French doors with curtains divide the living room from the
bedrooms, but don't provide much privacy.

The **Red Star Tavern and Roast House** is a popular and traditionally styled restaurant specializing in upscale American comfort
food.

506 SW Washington St., Portland, OR 97204. ✆ **800/711-2971** or 503/222-0001.
Fax 503/222-0004. www.5thavenuesuites.com. 221 units. $139–$169 double;
$169–$300 suite. AE, DC, DISC, MC, V. Valet parking $21. **Amenities:** Restaurant
(American), lounge; pool; exercise room; Aveda day spa; concierge; business center;
24-hr. room service; laundry/dry cleaning. *In room:* A/C, TV, fax, dataport, minibar,
coffeemaker, hair dryer, iron.

Governor Hotel 𝒜𝒜𝒜   This historic hotel pays homage to the
Lewis and Clark Expedition, and you'll spot references to the

famous explorers throughout. However, the historical references are just the icing on the cake at this plush hotel.

Guest rooms vary considerably in size but are all attractively decorated, with perks such as two-line phones and voice mail. The least expensive rooms are rather small but are nevertheless very comfortable. Still, we'd opt for one of the deluxe guest rooms. Unfortunately, bathrooms are, in general, quite cramped by today's standards and lack counter space, although their tile work does give them a classic feel. Suites, on the other hand, are spacious, and some even have huge patios overlooking the city.

Be sure to take a peek at the Dome Room, which is just off the lobby and has a stunning stained-glass skylight. Jake's Grill, a large, old-fashioned restaurant located just off the lobby, serves grilled steak and seafood. There's also a complimentary evening wine tasting Monday through Thursday.

611 SW 10th Ave., Portland, OR 97205. ⓒ **800/554-3456** or 503/224-3400. Fax 503/241-2122. www.govhotel.com. 100 units. $165–$195 double; $200 junior suite; $210–$500 suite. AE, DC, DISC, MC, V. Valet parking $16. **Amenities:** Restaurant (American), lounge; pool; access to adjacent health club with indoor pool, Jacuzzi, saunas, indoor running track; concierge; business center; 24-hr. room service; laundry service; dry cleaning. *In room:* A/C, TV, dataport, minibar, coffeemaker, hair dryer, iron.

The Heathman Hotel ⓐⓐⓐ   With its understated luxury and superb service, The Heathman is one of the finest hotels in the city. Although primarily a top-end business hotel, it's also the address of choice for visiting culture hounds, with its proximity to the theater and an outstanding collection of art ranging from 18th-century oil paintings to Andy Warhol prints. Don't look for a bowl-you-over lobby here; although there is plenty of marble and teak, the lobby itself is tiny. However, just off the lobby is the Tea Court, where the original eucalyptus paneling creates a warm, old-world atmosphere.

The basic rooms here tend to be quite small, but are nonetheless attractively furnished and set up for business travelers. There are no real views to speak of, but rooms on the west side of the hotel look out to a mural done just for the hotel. Basically what you get here is luxury in a small space. The corner rooms are lighter and more spacious.

The **Heathman Restaurant** is one of Portland's finest (see the review on p. 60). Afternoon tea is served in the Lobby Lounge, and there's usually live jazz nightly. There are also complimentary wine tastings several nights a week.

1001 SW Broadway at Salmon St., Portland, OR 97205. ⓒ **800/551-0011** or 503/ 241-4100. Fax 503/790-7110. www.heathmanhotel.com. 150 units. $169–$209 double; $305–$775 suite. AE, DC, DISC, MC, V. Parking $19. Pets accepted for $25. **Amenities:** Restaurant (Northwest), lounge; exercise room, access to nearby health club; concierge; room service; laundry service; dry cleaning. *In room:* A/C, TV, dataport, minibar, coffeemaker, hair dryer, iron, high-speed Internet access.

Hotel Vintage Plaza ⭒⭒

This hotel, which was built in 1894 and is on the National Register of Historic Places, is *the* place to stay in Portland if you are a wine lover. A wine theme predominates in the hotel's decor, and there are complimentary evening tastings of Northwest wines. There are a wide variety of room types here, and though the standard rooms are worth recommending, the starlight rooms and bi-level suites are the real scene-stealers. The starlight rooms in particular are truly extraordinary. Though small, they have greenhouse-style wall-to-ceiling windows that provide very romantic views at night and let in floods of light during the day. The bi-level suites, some with Japanese soaking tubs and one with a spiral staircase, are equally attractive spaces.

Pazzo Ristorante, one of Portland's best Italian restaurants, is a dark, intimate trattoria.

422 SW Broadway, Portland, OR 97205. ⓒ **800/243-0555** or 503/228-1212. Fax 503/228-3598. www.vintageplaza.com. 107 units. $150–$225 double; $325–$400 suite. AE, DC, DISC, MC, V. Valet parking $21. Pets accepted. **Amenities:** Restaurant (Italian), lounge; exercise room, access to nearby health club; concierge; business center; 24-hr. room service; massage; laundry service; same-day dry cleaning. *In room:* A/C, TV, fax, dataport, minibar, hair dryer, iron.

Portland Marriott Downtown ⭒⭒

Located just across Waterfront Park and Naito Parkway from the Willamette River, the high-rise Portland Marriott offers great views of Mount Hood from its upper east-side rooms, and this alone would be reason enough to stay here. That the park across the street serves as the site of virtually all of Portland's main festivals also makes it a good choice if you're in town for one of these festivals. (If you're planning a weekend visit, be sure to find out if there's a festival scheduled; depending on your interest in the event, you'll either find this to be a great location, or you might not want to deal with the crowds.) Otherwise, this standard corporate high-rise doesn't have a whole lot of character, though there is a nice Japanese-style garden outside the front door. Most of the guest rooms have small balconies, and if you ask for a room overlooking the river, throw back the glass door to the balcony and think about the fact that the view used to be of a noisy freeway (it was torn out to build the park). All the rooms have been recently redone.

1401 SW Naito Pkwy., Portland, OR 97201. ✆ **800/228-9290** or 503/226-7600. Fax 503/221-1789. www.marriott.com/htls/pdxor. 503 units. $114–$199 double; $450–$600 suite. AE, DC, DISC, MC, V. Valet parking $19. Pets accepted with $50 nonrefundable fee. **Amenities:** 2 restaurants (American), 2 lounges (1 sports bar, 1 more sedate lobby lounge); indoor pool; exercise room; Jacuzzi; sauna; concierge; business center; room service; coin-op laundry; laundry service; dry cleaning; concierge level. *In room:* A/C, TV, dataport, coffeemaker, hair dryer, iron.

MODERATE

Doubletree Portland Downtown 𝄢𝄢

Situated on a shady tree-lined street about a mile south of Pioneer Courthouse Square and on the southern edge of downtown Portland, this low-rise hotel offers the convenience of a downtown location and the casual appeal of a suburban business hotel. The design and landscaping reflect the Northwest, and in the courtyard surrounding the swimming pool are lush plantings of evergreens and other shrubs. Keep in mind that in summer, this hotel only qualifies for the inexpensive category on weekends. The best rooms are those on the third floor overlooking the pool courtyard. Although slightly more expensive, these rooms are quiet and have pleasant views. They also get plenty of that precious Northwest sunlight (when the sun shines), although all the rooms have large windows.

310 SW Lincoln St., Portland, OR 97201. ✆ **800/222-TREE** or 503/221-0450. Fax 503/226-6260. www.doubletreehotels.com. 235 units. $79–$149 double; $200–$400 suite. AE, DC, DISC, MC, V. Parking $10. Pets accepted with $25 deposit. **Amenities:** Restaurant (American), lounge; outdoor pool; exercise room; concierge; room service; laundry/dry cleaning. *In room:* A/C, TV, coffeemaker, hair dryer.

Downtown Portland's Imperial Hotel 𝄢 *Value*

Although it doesn't quite live up to its regal name, this remodeled older hotel across the street from the Benson is a good bet for moderately priced accommodations at a great downtown location. Although the staff may be young and not as polished as those at more expensive hotels, they usually are good about seeing to guests' needs. Rooms are quite up-to-date. The corner king rooms, with large windows, should be your first choice; barring this, ask for an exterior room. These might get a little street noise, but they're bigger than the interior rooms and get more sunlight. Free local calls are a nice perk.

400 SW Broadway, Portland, OR 97205. ✆ **800/452-2323** or 503/228-7221. Fax 503/223-4551. www.hotel-imperial.com. 128 units. $90–$130 double. Rates include continental breakfast. AE, DC, DISC, MC, V. Valet parking $15. Pets accepted with $10 fee. **Amenities:** Highly regarded restaurant (Thai), lounge with live jazz; access to nearby health club; dry cleaning. *In room:* A/C, TV, dataport, fridge, hair dryer, iron, safe.

Four Points Hotel Sheraton ★★ *Value*   Overlooking Waterfront Park and located on the MAX light-rail line, this 1960s vintage hotel is nondescript from the outside, but the inside has been renovated with a contemporary look that makes it one of the most stylish hotels in town. You are only steps from the Willamette River (although not actually on the water), and are also close to businesses, fine restaurants, and shopping. Guest rooms are as boldly contemporary in design as the lobby and restaurant, which are sort of downscale *Architectural Digest.*

50 SW Morrison St., Portland, OR 97204-3390. ✆ **800/899-0247** or 503/221-0711. Fax 503/274-0312. www.fourpointsportland.com. 140 units. $99–$140 double. AE, DC, DISC, MC, V. Parking $10. Pets accepted. **Amenities:** Restaurant (American/international), lounge; access to nearby health club; room service; massage; dry cleaning. *In room:* A/C, TV, dataport, coffeemaker, hair dryer, iron.

Mallory Hotel ★ *Finds*   The Mallory, which is right on the westside Max line, has long been a favorite of Portland visitors who want the convenience of staying downtown but aren't on a bottomless expense account. This is an older hotel, and the lobby, with its ornate gilt plasterwork trim and crystal chandeliers, has a certain classic (and faded) grandeur. Time seems to have stood still here. (There's a lounge straight out of the 1950s.)

The standard rooms are not as luxurious as the lobby might suggest and are smaller than comparable rooms at the Imperial or Days Inn, but are comfortable and clean. With rates this low, you might even want to go for one of the king-size suites, which are as big as they come, with walk-in closets, refrigerators, and sofa beds. Free local calls are a nice perk.

The dining room continues the lobby's grand design, with heavy drapes and faux-marble pillars.

729 SW 15th Ave., Portland, OR 97205-1994. ✆ **800/228-8657** or 503/223-6311. Fax 503/223-0522. www.malloryhotel.com. 130 units. $95–$160 double; $160 suite. AE, DC, DISC, MC, V. Free parking. Pets accepted with $10 fee. **Amenities:** Restaurant (American), lounge; access to nearby health club; concierge; room service. *In room:* A/C, TV, dataport, fridge, iron, safe.

The Mark Spencer Hotel ★   If you're planning an extended stay in Portland and need to be right downtown, this is the place for you.

Although the hotel is not in the best neighborhood (there are lots of nightclubs and bars in the vicinity), it's just around the corner from both Powell's City of Books and Jake's Famous Crawfish, one of Portland's oldest and best seafood restaurants. The rooms and suites here have rather dated decor but all have kitchenettes, which is the main draw here for people planning on spending a week or more in town. The hotel offers afternoon tea, and there's also a great rooftop garden deck. The Mark Spencer is a favorite with the casts of touring Broadway shows, and is also a good choice for any gay travelers interested in checking out the nearby bars.

409 SW 11th Ave., Portland, OR 97205. © **800/548-3934** or 503/224-3293. Fax 503/223-7848. www.markspencer.com. 101 units. $89–$109 double; $109–$129 suite. Rates include continental breakfast. AE, DC, MC, V. Free parking. Pets accepted with $25 nonrefundable deposit. **Amenities:** Access to nearby health club; coin-op laundry; laundry service; dry cleaning. *In room:* A/C, TV, dataport, kitchen, fridge, coffeemaker.

2 Nob Hill & Northwest Portland

EXPENSIVE

Heron Haus ☆☆   A short walk from the bustling Nob Hill shopping and dining district of northwest Portland, the Heron Haus B&B offers outstanding accommodations, spectacular views, and tranquil surroundings. Surprisingly, the house still features some of the original plumbing. In most places this would be a liability, but not here, since the same man who plumbed Portland's famous Pittock Mansion (p. 91) did the plumbing here. Many of that building's unusual bathroom features are also found at the Heron Haus—one shower has *seven* showerheads. In another room there's a modern whirlpool spa with excellent views of the city. All the rooms have fireplaces.

2545 NW Westover Rd., Portland, OR 97210. © **503/274-1846.** Fax 503/248-4055. www.heronhaus.com. 6 units. $135–$350 double. Rates include continental breakfast. MC, V. Free parking. *In room:* A/C, TV, dataport, hair dryer, iron.

MODERATE

Silver Cloud Inn Portland Downtown ☆   This hotel is on the edge of Portland's trendy Nob Hill neighborhood, and though it faces the beginning of the city's industrial area, it is still a very attractive and comfortable place (ask for a room away from Vaughn St.). Reasonable rates are the main draw here, but the rooms are also well-designed and filled with plenty of conveniences, such as free local calls. Although the minisuites have wet bars, microwave ovens,

Kids   Family-Friendly Hotels

Embassy Suites (*p. 43*)   Located in the center of the city, this renovated historic hotel offers spacious rooms (mostly two-room suites). You and the kids will have room to spread out and can hang out by the indoor pool when you tire of exploring Portland.

Homewood Suites by Hilton Vancouver/Portland (*p. 53*) Although this hotel is across the Columbia River in Vancouver, Washington, its location right across the street from the river, a paved riverside trail, a fun family restaurant, and a brewpub all add up to convenience for families. That you'll get a one- or two-bedroom apartment with a full kitchen just makes life on vacation that much easier.

The Lakeshore Inn (*p. 56*)   This reasonably priced inn is right on the shore of the lake and it also has a pool. The big rooms with kitchenettes are great for families; for more space, opt for a one- or two-bedroom suite.

and separate seating areas, the king rooms with whirlpool tubs, which happen to be the most expensive rooms, are our favorites. However, the best thing about the hotel is its location within a 5-minute drive (or 15-min. walk) of a half dozen of the city's best restaurants. To find the hotel, take I-405 to Ore. 30 west and get off at the Vaughn Street exit.

2426 NW Vaughn St., Portland, OR 97210. ℂ **800/205-6939** or 503/242-2400. Fax 503/242-1770. www.silvercloud.com. 83 units. $89–$139 double. Rates include continental breakfast. AE, DC, DISC, MC, V. Free parking. **Amenities:** Exercise room; Jacuzzi; business center; coin-op laundry; laundry service; dry cleaning. *In room:* A/C, TV, dataport, coffeemaker, hair dryer, iron.

3 The Rose Quarter & Irvington
EXPENSIVE
The Lion and the Rose 🏅🏅   This imposing Queen Anne–style Victorian inn is located in the Irvington District, a fairly quiet residential neighborhood 1 block off Northeast Broadway. It's a good choice if you want to keep your driving to a minimum. Restaurants, cafes, eclectic boutiques, and a huge shopping mall are all within

4 blocks. Even without the splendid location, the inn would be a gem. Guest rooms each have a distinctively different decor. In the Lavonna room, there are bright colors and a turret sitting area, while in the deep green Starina room you'll find an imposing Edwardian bed and armoire. Both the Garden room and the Lavonna Room's shared bathroom have claw-foot tubs, while some rooms have rather cramped, though attractive, bathrooms. If you have problems climbing stairs, ask for the ground floor's Rose room, which has a whirlpool tub. Breakfasts are sumptuous affairs, great for lingering.

1810 NE 15th Ave., Portland, OR 97212. ⓒ **800/955-1647** or 503/287-9245. Fax 503/287-9247. www.lionrose.com. 6 units, 1 with shared bathroom. $95–$140 double. AE, DISC, MC, V. **Amenities:** Concierge. *In room:* A/C, TV, hair dryer, iron.

MODERATE

McMenamins Kennedy School ⭐⭐ *(Finds)*   The Kennedy School is from the same folks who turned Portland's old poor farm into the most entertaining and unusual B&B in the state (see the listing for McMenamins Edgefield on p. 54 in this chapter). This inn, located well north of stylish Irvington in an up-and-coming neighborhood that dates from the early years of the 20th century, was an elementary school from 1915 to 1975. In the guest rooms you'll still find the original blackboards and great big school clocks (you know, like the one you used to watch so expectantly). However, the classroom/guest rooms here now have their own bathrooms, so you won't have to raise your hand or walk down the hall. On the premises you'll also find a restaurant, a beer garden, a movie theater pub, a cigar bar, and a big hot soaking pool.

5736 NE 33rd Ave., Portland, OR 97211. ⓒ **888/249-3983** or 503/249-3983. www. mcmenamins.com. 35 units. $99–$109 double. Rates include full breakfast. AE, DISC, MC, V. **Amenities:** Restaurant (American), 5 lounges; soaking pool; massage. *In room:* Dataport.

Portland's White House ⭐⭐   With massive columns framing the entrance, semicircular driveway, and in the front garden, a bubbling fountain, this imposing Greek-revival mansion bears a more than passing resemblance to its namesake in Washington, D.C. Behind the mahogany front doors, a huge entrance hall with original hand-painted wall murals is flanked by a parlor, with French windows and a piano, and the formal dining room, where the large breakfast is served beneath sparkling crystal chandeliers. A double staircase leads past a large stained-glass window to the second-floor accommodations. Canopy and brass queen beds, antique furnishings, and bathrooms with claw-foot tubs further the feeling of

classic luxury here. Request the balcony room, and you can gaze out past the Greek columns and imagine you're in the Oval Office. There are also three rooms in the restored carriage house.

1914 NE 22nd Ave., Portland, OR 97212. © **800/272-7131** or 503/287-7131. Fax 503/249-1641. www.portlandswhitehouse.com. 9 units. $98–$169 double. Rates include full breakfast. AE, DISC, MC, V. *In room:* A/C, dataport, fridge, hair dryer, iron.

INEXPENSIVE

Sullivan's Gulch B&B ⪡   Set on a quiet, tree-shaded street just a couple blocks from busy Northeast Broadway, this inn is a 1907 home filled with an eclectic mix of Mission-style furniture, Asian artifacts, and contemporary art. Our favorite room here is the Northwest Room, which is decorated with Northwest Coast Native-American masks and has an old Hudson's Bay Company blanket on the bed. There's also a room that draws on Montana and Western art for its decor. A pretty little deck out back is a pleasant place to hang out in summer. The inn is popular with gay and lesbian travelers, and with the MAX stop just a few blocks away it's convenient to downtown.

1744 NE Clackamas St., Portland, OR 97232. © **503/331-1104.** Fax 503/331-1575. www.sullivansgulch.com. 4 units, 2 with shared bathroom. $70–$85 double. AE, MC, V. Pets accepted. *In room:* TV, fridge, no phone.

4 Jantzen Beach (North Portland) & Vancouver, Washington

Located on Hayden Island in the middle of the Columbia River, Jantzen Beach, named for the famous swimwear company that got its start here, is a beach in name only. Today this area is a huge shopping mall complex aimed primarily at Washingtonians, who come to Oregon to avoid Washington's sales tax. Jantzen Beach is also home to a pair of large convention hotels that are among the city's only waterfront hotels. Both hotels are, however, in the flight path for the airport, and although the rooms themselves are adequately insulated against noise, the swimming pools and sun decks can be pretty noisy.

MODERATE

Doubletree Hotel Portland Columbia River ⪡⪡   Attractive landscaping and an interesting low-rise design that's somewhat reminiscent of a Northwest Coast Indian longhouse give this convention hotel a resort-like feel and have kept it popular for many years.

Although rush-hour traffic problems can make this a bad choice if you're here to explore Portland, it's a good location if you plan to visit Mount St. Helens. Guest rooms are large, though rather nondescript. Be sure to ask for one of the rooms with a view of the Columbia River.

1401 N. Hayden Island Dr., Portland, OR 97217. ⓒ **800/222-TREE** or 503/283-2111. Fax 503/283-4718. www.doubletreehotels.com. 351 units. $100–$125 double; $200–$250 suite. AE, DC, DISC, MC, V. Free parking. Pets accepted with $30 nonrefundable deposit. **Amenities:** 2 restaurants (Northwest, American), 2 lounges; outdoor pool; access to exercise room at adjacent hotel; Jacuzzi; concierge; courtesy airport shuttle; room service; laundry/dry cleaning. *In room:* A/C, TV, dataport, coffeemaker, hair dryer, iron.

The Heathman Lodge ⭐⭐ *Value* Mountain lodge meets urban chic at this suburban Vancouver hotel adjacent to the Vancouver Mall, and though it's a 20-minute drive to downtown Portland, the hotel is well placed for exploring both the Columbia Gorge and Mount St. Helens. With its log, stone, and cedar-shingle construction, this hotel conjures up the Northwest's historic mountain lodges and is filled with artwork and embellished with rugged Northwest-inspired craftwork, including totem poles, Eskimo kayak frames, and Pendleton blankets. Guest rooms feature a mix of rustic pine and peeled-hickory furniture.

7801 NE Greenwood Dr., Vancouver, WA 98662. ⓒ **888/475-3100** or 360/254-3100. Fax 360/254-6100. www.heathmanlodge.com. 143 units. $89–$139 double; $159–$550 suite. AE, DC, DISC, MC, V. Free parking. **Amenities:** Restaurant (Northwest), lounge; indoor pool; exercise room; Jacuzzi; sauna; concierge; business center; room service; guest laundry; laundry service; dry cleaning. *In room:* A/C, TV, dataport, fridge, coffeemaker, hair dryer, iron, microwave.

Homewood Suites by Hilton Vancouver/Portland ⭐⭐ *Kids* Located across the street from the Columbia River, this modern suburban all-suite hotel is a great choice for families. The hotel charges surprisingly reasonable rates for large apartment-like accommodations that include full kitchens. Rates include not only a large breakfast, but afternoon snacks as well (Mon–Thurs). These snacks are substantial enough to pass for dinner if you aren't too hungry. The hotel is right across the street from both a beach-theme restaurant and a brewpub. Across the street, you'll also find a paved riverside path that's great for walking or jogging. The only drawback is that it's a 15- to 20-minute drive to downtown Portland.

701 SE Columbia Shores Blvd., Vancouver, WA 98661. © 800/CALL-HOME or 360/750-1100. Fax 360/750-4899. www.homewood-suites.com. 104 units. $99–$119 double. Rates include full breakfast. AE, DC, DISC, MC, V. Free parking. Pets accepted with $25 nonrefundable deposit plus $10 per night. **Amenities:** Outdoor pool; exercise room; Jacuzzi; sports court; business center; coin-op laundry. *In room:* A/C, TV, dataport, kitchen, fridge, coffeemaker, hair dryer, iron.

5 The Airport Area & Troutdale

Moderately priced hotels have been proliferating in the airport area in the past few years, which makes this a good place to look for a room if you arrive with no reservation.

EXPENSIVE

Shilo Inn Suites Hotel Portland Airport ★★   If you need to stay near the airport and want a spacious room and the facilities of a deluxe hotel, this is one of your best bets. The rooms are spacious and have many amenities such as large closets with mirrored doors, lots of bathroom counter space, double sinks, and three TVs (including one in the bathroom). The main drawback here is that this is a convention hotel and is often very crowded. To find the Shilo, head straight out of the airport, drive under the I-205 overpass, and watch for the hotel ahead on the left.

11707 NE Airport Way, Portland, OR 97220-1075. © **800/222-2244** or 503/252-7500. Fax 503/254-0794. www.shiloinns.com. 200 units. $79–$169 double. Rates include full breakfast. AE, DC, DISC, MC, V. Free parking. **Amenities:** Restaurant (American), lounge; indoor pool; exercise room; Jacuzzi; sauna; tour desk; courtesy airport shuttle; business center; room service; coin-op laundry; dry cleaning. *In room:* A/C, TV, dataport, fridge, coffeemaker, hair dryer, iron, safe.

MODERATE

McMenamins Edgefield ★ *Finds*   B&Bs don't usually have more than 100 rooms, but this is no ordinary inn. Located 30 minutes east of downtown Portland and ideally situated for exploring the Columbia Gorge and Mount Hood, this flagship of the McMenamin microbrewery empire is the former Multnomah County poor farm. Today the property includes not only tastefully decorated guest rooms with antique furnishings, but a brewery, a pub, a beer garden, a restaurant, a movie theater, a winery, a wine-tasting room, a distillery, a golf course, a cigar bar in an old shed, and extensive gardens. With so much in one spot, this makes a great base for exploring the area. The beautiful grounds give this inn the feel of a remote retreat, though you're still within a short drive of everything Portland has to offer.

2126 SW Halsey St., Troutdale, OR 97060. ℂ 800/669-8610 or 503/669-8610. Fax 5-3/492-7750. www.mcmenamins.com. 114 units, 101 with shared bathroom; 24 hostel beds. $85–$105 double with shared bathroom, $115–$130 double with private bathroom; $20 hostel bed per person. Rates include full breakfast (not included with hostel). AE, DISC, MC, V. **Amenities:** 3 restaurants (Northwest, American), 6 lounges; 18-hole par-3 golf course; exercise room and access to nearby health club; Jacuzzi; sauna; business center; massage. *In room:* No phone.

Silver Cloud Inn Portland Airport 🐾 *Value*   Conveniently located right outside the airport, this hotel has one of the best backyards of any hotel in the Portland area. A lake, lawns, and trees create a tranquil setting despite the proximity of both the airport and a busy nearby road. Rooms are designed primarily for business travelers, but even if you aren't here on an expense account, they are a good value, especially those with whirlpool tubs (and you even get free local calls). Some suites have gas fireplaces. Best of all, with the exception of two suites, every room has a view of the lake. An indoor pool is another big plus. To find this hotel, take the complimentary airport shuttle or head straight out of the airport, drive under the I-205 overpass, and watch for the hotel sign ahead on the left.

11518 NE Glenn Widing Dr., Portland, OR 97220. ℂ 800/205-7892 or 503/ 252-2222. Fax 503/257-7008. www.silvercloud.com. 102 units. $89–$105 double; $129–$139 suite. Rates include continental breakfast. AE, DC, DISC, MC, V. Free parking. **Amenities:** Indoor pool; exercise room; Jacuzzi; courtesy airport shuttle; business center; coin-op laundry; dry cleaning. *In room:* A/C, TV, dataport, fridge, coffeemaker, hair dryer, iron, microwave, free local calls.

INEXPENSIVE

The **Super 8 Motel,** 11011 NE Holman St. (ℂ **503/257-8988**), just off Airport Way after you go under the I-205 overpass, is convenient but charges a surprisingly high $66 to $81 a night for a double in summer. Also not far away, in Troutdale, at the mouth of the Columbia Gorge, you'll find a **Motel 6,** 1610 NW Frontage Rd., Troutdale (ℂ **503/665-2254**), charging $43 to $52 per night for a double.

6 The Southwest Suburbs (Lake Oswego & Beaverton)

MODERATE

Greenwood Inn 🐾🐾   The Greenwood Inn is a resortlike, low-rise hotel with beautifully landscaped grounds that reflect the garden style of the Pacific Northwest. This is Beaverton's best hotel and is located only 15 to 20 minutes from downtown Portland. A good restaurant and an atmospheric lounge make this an all-around good choice. If you're in the area to do business in the "Silicon Forest," the Greenwood is a good location. Guest rooms are large and comfortable and most are designed with business travelers in mind, and in the bathrooms, you'll find plenty of counter space for toiletries. Executive rooms, which cost a little extra, are exceptional, with original artwork on the walls, three phones, and a well-lighted desk/work area.

10700 SW Allen Blvd., Beaverton, OR 97005. ☎ **800/289-1300** or 503/643-7444. Fax 503/626-4553. www.greenwoodinn.com. 251 units. $79–$118 double; $150–$375 suite. AE, DC, DISC, MC, V. Free parking. Pets accepted with $25 fee. **Amenities:** Restaurant (Italian), lounge; 2 outdoor pools; exercise room and access to nearby health club; Jacuzzi; sauna; business center; room service; coin-op laundry; laundry service; dry cleaning. *In room:* A/C, TV, dataport, fridge, coffeemaker, hair dryer, iron.

INEXPENSIVE

The Lakeshore Inn ★ *Finds* *Kids*   Considering that the town of Lake Oswego is Portland's most affluent bedroom community, this motel is quite reasonably priced. It's right on the shore of the lake, and there's a pool on a deck built on the water's edge, making it a great place to stay in summer. Rooms have standard motel furnishings but are large and have kitchenettes. There are also one- and two-bedroom suites. The 7-mile drive into downtown Portland follows the Willamette River and is quite pleasant. There are several restaurants and cafes within walking distance.

210 N. State St., Lake Oswego, OR 97034. ☎ **800/215-6431** or 503/636-9679. Fax 503/636-6959. www.thelakeshoreinn.com. 33 units. $69–$99 double; $89–$129 suite. AE, DC, DISC, MC, V. **Amenities:** Outdoor pool; access to nearby health club; coin-op laundry. *In room:* A/C, TV, dataport, kitchenette, coffeemaker, hair dryer, iron.

5

Where to Dine

In the past few years the Portland restaurant scene has gotten so hot that the city is beginning to develop a Seattle-style reputation. Excellent new restaurants keep popping up around the city. Several distinct dining districts are full of upscale spots, and though you aren't likely to choose to eat at one of these places on the spur of the moment (reservations are usually imperative), their proximity allows you to check out a few places before making a decision for later.

The Pearl District's renovated warehouses currently house the trendiest restaurants, while Nob Hill's Northwest 21st Avenue boasts half a dozen terrific establishments within a few blocks. The Sellwood and Westmoreland neighborhoods of Southeast Portland make up another of the city's hot restaurant districts, and for good inexpensive food, it's hard to beat the many offerings along NE Broadway in the Irvington neighborhood.

Dinner in Portland isn't complete without an Oregon wine. Pinot Noir and Pinot Gris in particular receive widespread acclaim. However, they can be more expensive than other domestic wines.

1 Downtown (Including the Skidmore Historic District & Chinatown)

VERY EXPENSIVE

Couvron ✸✸✸ CONTEMPORARY FRENCH If you're in Portland for a very special occasion and are looking for the most memorable restaurant in town, this is it. Located in the Goose Hollow neighborhood at the foot of the West Hills and only a few blocks from the PGE Park baseball stadium, this diminutive restaurant has an utterly unremarkable facade yet a thoroughly French and unpretentiously sophisticated interior. The menu is one of the most extraordinary in the city, featuring fine ingredients in unusual flavor combinations that almost always hit the mark. Dinners here are multicourse affairs that change with the seasons. Expect such interesting creations as an ahi salad with avocado, fresh wasabi, and citrus vinaigrette; chilled tomato soup; smoked quail with organic

Where to Dine in Portland

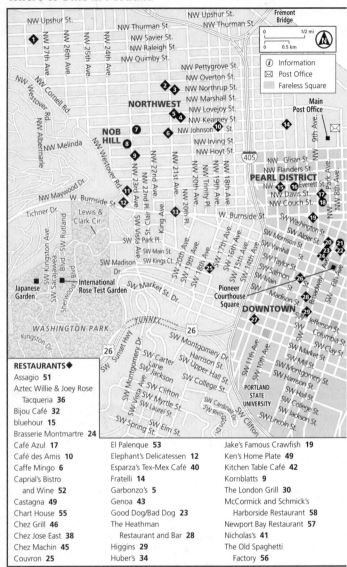

RESTAURANTS◆

Assagio **51**

Aztec Willie & Joey Rose
  Tacqueria **36**

Bijou Café **32**

bluehour **15**

Brasserie Montmartre **24**

Café Azul **17**

Café des Amis **10**

Caffe Mingo **6**

Caprial's Bistro
  and Wine **52**

Castagna **49**

Chart House **55**

Chez Grill **46**

Chez Jose East **38**

Chez Machin **45**

Couvron **25**

El Palenque **53**

Elephant's Delicatessen **12**

Esparza's Tex-Mex Café **40**

Fratelli **14**

Garbonzo's **5**

Genoa **43**

Good Dog/Bad Dog **23**

The Heathman
  Restaurant and Bar **28**

Higgins **29**

Huber's **34**

Jake's Famous Crawfish **19**

Ken's Home Plate **49**

Kitchen Table Café **42**

Kornblatts **9**

The London Grill **30**

McCormick and Schmick's
  Harborside Restaurant **58**

Newport Bay Restaurant **57**

Nicholas's **41**

The Old Spaghetti
  Factory **56**

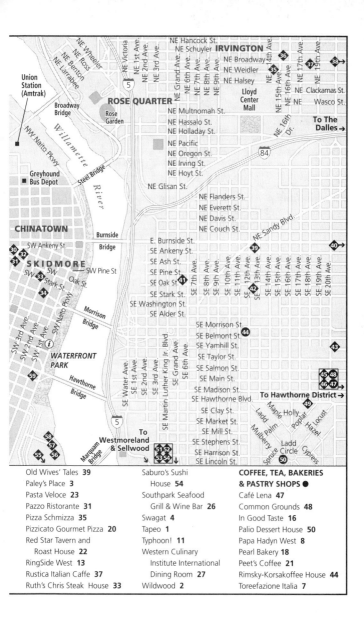

Old Wives' Tales **39**	Saburo's Sushi
Paley's Place **3**	House **54**
Pasta Veloce **23**	Southpark Seafood
Pazzo Ristorante **31**	Grill & Wine Bar **26**
Pizza Schmizza **35**	Swagat **4**
Pizzicato Gourmet Pizza **20**	Tapeo **1**
Red Star Tavern and	Typhoon! **11**
Roast House **22**	Western Culinary
RingSide West **13**	Institute International
Rustica Italian Caffe **37**	Dining Room **27**
Ruth's Chris Steak House **33**	Wildwood **2**

**COFFEE, TEA, BAKERIES
& PASTRY SHOPS ●**

Café Lena **47**
Common Grounds **48**
In Good Taste **16**
Palio Dessert House **50**
Papa Hadyn West **8**
Pearl Bakery **18**
Peet's Coffee **21**
Rimsky-Korsakoffee House **44**
Toreefazione Italia **7**

fingerling potatoes, truffles, truffle oil, and wine sauce; saddle of rabbit with lentils and sautéed foie gras; and lobster with polenta, corn, chanterelles and port-wine sauce.

1126 SW 18th Ave. ℭ 503/225-1844. www.couvron.com. Reservations required. Prix fixe menus only: $65 (vegetarian), $75, or $95. AE, MC, V. Tues–Sat 5:30–9pm.

EXPENSIVE

In addition to the restaurants listed below, two high-end steakhouse chains—**Ruth's Chris Steak House,** 309 SW Third Ave. (ℭ **503/ 221-4518**) and **Morton's,** 213 SW Clay St. (ℭ **503/248-2005**)— both have restaurants in downtown Portland.

The Heathman Restaurant and Bar 🟊🟊🟊 NORTHWEST/ FRENCH This grande dame of Northwest-style restaurants serves Northwest cuisine with a French accent, and in 2001, executive chef Philippe Boulot received the James Beard Foundation's "Best Chef in the Northwest" award. Boulot's menu changes seasonally, but one thing remains constant: The ingredients used are the very freshest of Oregon and Northwest seafood, meat, wild game, and produce. The interior is Art Deco inspired, the atmosphere bistro-like. The menu changes daily and is quite extensive. We advise picking appetizers and entrees from the "Northwest Specialties" lists, but the dishes from the grill are also good choices. The bar offers Northwest microbrewery beers on tap, while an extensive wine list spotlights Oregon wines.

The Heathman Hotel has an extensive collection of classic and contemporary art, and on the restaurant walls you'll find Andy Warhol's *Endangered Species* series.

In the Heathman Hotel, 1001 SW Broadway. ℭ 503/790-7758. Reservations highly recommended. Main courses $7.25–$15 at lunch, $16–$30 at dinner. AE, DC, MC, V. Mon–Fri 6:30–11am and 11:30am–2pm; Sat–Sun 7am–2pm; Mon–Thurs 5–10pm; Fri–Sat 5–11pm.

Higgins 🟊🟊🟊 NORTHWEST/MEDITERRANEAN Higgins, located just up Broadway from the Heathman Hotel, where chef Greg Higgins first made a name for himself in Portland, strikes a balance between contemporary and classic in both decor and cuisine. The menu, which changes frequently, explores contemporary culinary horizons, while the decor in the tri-level dining room opts for wood paneling and elegant place settings. Yet despite all this, the restaurant remains unpretentious. Portions here can be surprisingly generous for a high-end restaurant. Flavors change with the season, but are often both subtle and earthy. A recent entree of roast pork loin with grilled sweet Walla Walla onions, cherry glace, and Swiss roesti-style potatoes highlighted the restaurant's ability to balance creativity with familiarity. Be sure to leave room for dessert, and if you happen to be a beer lover, you'll be glad to know that Higgins has one of the most interesting beer selections in town (plenty of good wine, too).

1239 SW Broadway. © **503/222-9070.** Reservations recommended. Main courses $7.75–$13.75 at lunch, $16.50–$26.50 at dinner. AE, DC, MC, V. Mon–Fri 11:30am–2pm and 5–10:30pm; Sat–Sun 5–10:30pm; bistro menu served in the bar daily until midnight.

The London Grill ⋇⋇⋇ NORTHWEST/CONTINENTAL/ BREAKFAST/BRUNCH   When you really want to feel like a major player, there's only one place in Portland that will do. The London Grill, located below the lobby of the luxurious Benson Hotel, has long been one of Portland's top restaurants. The restaurant is modeled after the original London Grill, which was a favorite with Queen Elizabeth I. Vaulted ceilings give the restaurant a wine-cellar feel, while mahogany paneling reflects the glowing chandeliers. Service is impeccable, and both breakfast and lunch are popular with business executives.

The chef uses many of the Northwest's finest fresh fruits and vegetables in dishes such as salmon glazed with sake and ginger, veal medallions with brandy-paprika cream sauce, and chicken Wellington (stuffed with foie gras, roasted tomatoes, and mushrooms). The Sunday champagne brunch is the most elegant in the city (be sure to make reservations). There is also a wine cellar available for private dining.

In the Benson Hotel, 309 SW Broadway. © **503/228-2000.** Reservations highly recommended. Main courses $25–$40; Sun brunch $25.50. AE, DC, DISC, MC, V. Mon–Tues 6:30am–2pm and 5–9pm; Wed–Sat 6:30am–2pm and 5–10pm; Sun 9:30am–2pm (brunch) and 5–9pm.

Veritable Quandary ⋇⋇ NEW AMERICAN   Located in an old brick building just a block off Tom McCall Waterfront Park, this restaurant is a must for summer meals. The restaurant's garden patio, the prettiest in town, faces a small park. The menu changes daily, but keep an eye out for the grilled prawns, sometimes served with strawberries and green peppercorn sauce, and don't pass up the *osso buco.* The chef here pulls in all kinds of influences, so don't be surprised if you find grilled beef skewers with a Peruvian marinade or prosciutto with fig molasses, fresh figs, and warm bruschetta, or springs rolls filled with duck confit, shiitakes, and Chinese cabbage (served with a side of wasabi-ginger sauce).

1220 SW First Ave. ℭ 503/227-7342. Reservations recommended. Main courses $16–$25. AE, DC, DISC, MC, V. Mon–Fri 11:30am–3pm; Sat–Sun 9:30am–3:30pm; Sun–Thurs 5–10pm; Fri–Sat 5–11pm.

MODERATE

There's an outpost of **Typhoon!** at 400 SW Broadway (ℭ **503/224-8285**), in the Imperial Hotel. See the complete review on p. 69.

Brasserie Montmartre ℛ NORTHWEST/FRENCH/LATE-NIGHT DINING   Though the menu lacks the creativity of other Northwest and French restaurants in Portland, and dishes are sometimes disappointing, The Bra (as it's known) is popular for its fun atmosphere. There's live jazz nightly, and several nights each week, a magician performs amazing feats of digital dexterity. On every table you'll find a paper tablecloth and a container of crayons, so you can let your artistic ambitions run wild. This hip playfulness is balanced out by dark, formal dining rooms, with massive faux marble pillars, black-and-white tile floors, velvet banquettes, and silk lamp shades that lend an air of fin-de-siècle Paris. You might start your meal with a *ménage à trois* of patés, then have a cup of onion soup with three cheeses, move on to Oregon snapper with crabmeat and *beurre blanc*, and finish off with one of the divinely decadent pastries. The wine list is extensive and includes many reasonably priced choices.

626 SW Park Ave. ℭ 503/224-5552. www.brasseriemontmartre.com. Reservations recommended. Main courses $6–$12 at lunch, $12–$20 at dinner. AE, DC, MC, V. Daily 11am–2pm and 5–10pm; bistro menu available Sun–Thurs 2pm–1am and Fri–Sat 2pm–3am.

Huber's ℛ *(Finds)* AMERICAN   Huber's, Portland's oldest restaurant, first opened its doors to the public in 1879 and is tucked inside the Oregon Pioneer Building down a quiet hallway. The main room has a vaulted stained-glass ceiling, Philippine mahogany paneling, and the original brass cash register.

Turkey dinner with all the trimmings is the house specialty, but you can also gobble turkey enchiladas, turkey Parmesan, and even Moroccan turkey. Another specialty is Spanish coffee made with rum, Kahlúa, Triple Sec, coffee, and cream. The preparation, which involves flaming the rum in a wineglass, is a very impressive tableside production. Because Huber's bar is quite popular, you'll probably enjoy your meal more if you come for lunch instead of dinner. Be sure to ask for a table in the old vaulted room.

411 SW Third Ave. ℂ **503/228-5686.** www.hubers.com. Reservations recommended. Main courses $6–$20 at lunch, $8–$20 at dinner. AE, DC, DISC, MC, V. Mon–Thurs 11:30am–midnight; Fri 11:30am–1am; Sat noon–1am.

Jake's Famous Crawfish ⋒⋒ SEAFOOD Great seafood at reasonable prices make this place a winner. Jake's has been a Portland institution since 1909, and the back bar came all the way around Cape Horn in 1880. Much of the rest of the decor looks just as old and well worn as the bar and therein lies this restaurant's charm.

There's a daily menu listing a dozen or more specials, but there's really no question about what to eat at Jake's: crawfish, which are always on the menu and are served several different ways. Monday through Friday from 3 to 6pm, bar appetizers are only $1.95. The noise level after work, when local businesspeople pack the bar, can be high, and the wait for a table can be long if you don't make a reservation. However, don't let these obstacles put you off.

401 SW 12th Ave. ℂ **503/226-1419.** Reservations recommended. Main courses $5–$13 at lunch, $10–$43 at dinner. AE, DC, DISC, MC, V. Mon–Fri 11:30am–11pm; Sat 4–11pm; Sun 4–10pm.

McCormick and Schmick's Harborside Restaurant ⋒⋒ SEAFOOD Anchoring the opposite end of RiverPlace Esplanade from the RiverPlace Hotel, this large glitzy seafood restaurant serves up a view of the Willamette and excellent seafood. Four dining levels assure everyone a view of the river and marina below, and in summer, customers head out to tables on the Esplanade. Because it's so popular, the place tends to be noisy and the help can sometimes be a bit harried; however, this doesn't detract from the fine food. Although seafood (such as blackened cod with cilantro-lime butter or macadamia-encrusted mahimahi with tropical fruit salsa) is the main attraction here, the menu is quite extensive. The clientele is mostly upscale, especially at lunch and during the after-work hours.

0309 SW Montgomery St. ℂ **503/220-1865.** Reservations recommended. Main courses $9.75–$24. AE, DC, DISC, MC, V. Mon–Thurs 11am–10pm; Fri–Sat 11am–11pm; Sun 10am–3pm and 4–10pm.

Newport Bay Restaurant ⋒ *Kids* SEAFOOD Though there are Newport Bay restaurants all over the Portland area, this one has by far the best location—floating on the Willamette River. Located in the marina at Portland's beautiful RiverPlace shopping-and-dining complex, the Newport Bay provides excellent views of the river and the city skyline, especially from the deck. Popular with young couples, families, and boaters, this place exudes a cheery atmosphere, and service is efficient. Nearly everything on the menu has some sort of seafood in it, even the quiche, salads, and pastas. Entrees are straightforward and well prepared—nothing too fancy. Sunday brunch is a very good deal.

0425 SW Montgomery St. © 503/227-3474. www.newportbay.com. Reservations recommended. Main courses $10–$23; lunches and light main courses $6–$12. AE, DC, DISC, MC, V. Summer hours Mon–Thurs 11am–11pm; Fri–Sat 11am–midnight; Sun 10am–3pm (brunch) and 3–10pm. Closes 1 hr. earlier in winter.

Southpark Seafood Grill & Wine Bar 𝒜𝒜 *Value* MEDITER-
RANEAN/SEAFOOD   Can it be true? An upscale restaurant/ wine bar with downscale prices? Yes, that's exactly what you'll find here at Southpark (no relation to the TV show). So what's the catch? Wine prices are not as reasonable as the food prices, so what you save on your food bill, you'll probably spend on your wine. With its high ceiling, long heavy drapes, halogen lights, and interesting wall mural, the wine bar is a contemporary interpretation of a late-19th-century Parisian, and the main dining room is both comfortable and classy. For a starter, don't pass up the fried calamari served with salt-preserved lemons bursting with flavor. Equally delicious is the butternut squash and ricotta-filled ravioli with toasted hazelnuts, which comes in a rich Marsala wine sauce that begs to be sopped up with the crusty bread. An extensive wine list presents some compelling choices, and the desserts are consistently fine.

901 SW Salmon St. © 503/326-1300. www.southpark.citysearch.com. Reservations recommended. Main courses $8–$20. AE, DC, DISC, MC, V. Mon–Thurs 11:30am–midnight; Fri 11:30am–1am; Sat 11am–1am; Sun 10am–midnight.

INEXPENSIVE

Bijou Café 𝒜 NATURAL FOODS   The folks who run the Bijou take both food and health seriously. They'll serve you a bowl of steamed brown rice and raisins for breakfast, but you can also get delicious fresh oyster hash or brioche French toast. However, the real hits here are the sautéed potatoes and the muffins, which come with full breakfasts. Don't leave without trying them. Local and organic products are used as often as possible at this comfortably old-fashioned cafe.

132 SW Third Ave. © 503/222-3187. Breakfast and lunch $4–$9. MC, V. Mon–Fri 7am–2pm; Sat–Sun 8am–2pm.

Pasta Veloce 𝒜 ITALIAN   Pasta Veloce, which translates roughly as "noodles in a hurry," really lives up to its name—it's a quick, cheap place to get a tasty Italian meal downtown. Portions are not huge, but they are satisfying and come with rustic grilled bread. We really like the gnocchi with chicken, broccoli, and walnuts in a Gorgonzola sauce. Wine and beer are available at prices that match those of the pastas. There are two convenient locations.

933 SW Third Ave. (© 503/223-8200) and 1022 SW Morrison St. (© 503/916-4388). Main courses $5.25–$7.50. AE, DISC, MC, V. Third Ave. location Mon–Thurs 11am–8pm; Fri 11am–8:30pm; Sat noon–8:30pm. Morrison location Mon–Thurs 11:30am–9pm; Fri 11:30am–9:30pm; Sat noon–9:30pm.

Western Culinary Institute International Dining Room ☘

Value CONTINENTAL/AMERICAN   If you happen to be a frugal gourmet whose palate is more sophisticated than your wallet can afford, you'll want to schedule a meal here. The dining room serves five- to six-course gourmet meals prepared by advanced students at prices even a budget traveler can afford. The dining room decor is modern and unassuming, and the students who wait on you are eager to please. For each course you can choose from among two to half a dozen offerings. A sample dinner menu might begin with velouté Andalouse followed by sautéed vegetables in a puff pastry, a pear sorbet, grilled ahi tuna with black bean salsa, Chinese salad with smoked salmon, and mocha cheesecake. Remember, that's all for under $20! The five-course lunch for only $9.95 is an even better deal.

1316 SW 13th Ave. © 503/294-9770 or 800/666-0312. Reservations required. 5-course lunch $9.95; 6-course dinner $19.95; Thurs buffet $19.95. AE, MC, V. Tues–Fri 11:30am–1pm and 6–8pm.

2 Northwest Portland (Including the Pearl District & Nob Hill)

EXPENSIVE

bluehour ☘ FRENCH/ITALIAN   Restaurateur Bruce Carey has long dominated the Portland restaurant scene, and here at his latest high-style restaurant, he continues to woo and wow the local trendsetters. Despite the location in a recently converted warehouse that serves as headquarters for Portland advertising giant Wieden+Kennedy, bluehour has a very theatrical atmosphere. With sophisticated menu items such as pan-seared foie gras and smoked goose prosciutto, it's obvious that bluehour is issuing a challenge to Portland's other high-end restaurants. Unfortunately, the cacophonous noise level and tightly packed tables severely detract from the cultured cuisine. If you value conversation with your meal, steer clear of bluehour. This is definitely the sort of place where being seen by the right people is more important than the food.

250 NW 13th Ave. ✆ **503/226-3394**. www.bluehour.com. Reservations highly recommended. Main dishes $17.50–$30. AE, MC, V. Mon–Thurs 11:30am–2:30pm and 6–10pm; Fri 11:30am–2:30pm and 6–10:30pm; Sat 5:30–10:30pm.

Café Azul ⭐⭐ GOURMET MEXICAN Located in the Pearl District in what was clearly once an old warehouse, Café Azul is a long, narrow space softened by expanses of warm yellow and terra-cotta walls. The food here includes some of the best regional Mexican dishes you're likely to find this side of the border. Tasty margaritas are generous and can be made with a number of different tequilas; sangrita, a spicy nonalcoholic ancho chili and orange drink, also gets two thumbs up. Start by spreading some dangerously tasty chili butter on a crusty roll, then follow this with a taco sampler platter that includes handmade corn tortillas served with Yucatecan-style pork roasted in banana leaves. From Oaxaca, Mexico, comes the inspiration for Café Azul's *mole,* a rich, spicy sauce made with more than two-dozen ingredients, including toasted nuts, chocolate, and chilies, which might be served over chicken or duck. The house-made ice creams and sorbets, often made with unusual tropical fruits, are always a fitting finale. This may be expensive for Mexican food, but it's well worth it.

112 NW Ninth Ave. ✆ **503/525-4422**. Reservations recommended. Main courses $16.50–$25. DISC, MC, V. Tues–Thurs 5–9pm; Fri–Sat 5–9:30pm.

Paley's Place ⭐⭐ NORTHWEST/FRENCH Located in a Victorian-era house, Paley's is a favorite of Portland foodies. The menu ranges from traditional bistro fare to dishes with a hint of Northwest inspiration and relies extensively on the freshest local organic ingredients. Chef Vitaly Paley and his wife Kimberly run the show here and continue to receive accolades year after year. Whether you're in the mood for steamed mussels or something more unusual (pasta with chickpeas, preserved tuna, dried tuna roe, and mint), you'll certainly find something that appeals. If you've never tried sweetbreads, this is the place to do so, and the signature *frites,* with a mustard aïoli, are not to be missed. Big on wines, Paley's offers wine tasting on Wednesdays and an occasional winemaker dinner. For dessert, we can't pass up the warm chocolate soufflé with ice cream. In good weather, the front porch is the better place to dine. Inside, the restaurant is small and stylishly comfortable but can be quite noisy.

1204 NW 21st Ave. ℂ **503/243-2403.** www.paleysplace.citysearch.com. Reservations highly recommended. Main courses $15–$26. AE, MC, V. Mon–Thurs 5:30–10pm; Fri–Sat 5:30–11pm; Sun 5–10pm.

RingSide West ⟨★⟩ STEAK   Despite the location on a rather unattractive stretch of West Burnside Street, RingSide has long been a favorite Portland steak house. Boxing may be the main theme of the restaurant, but the name is a two-fisted pun that also refers to the incomparable onion rings that should be an integral part of any meal here. Have your rings with a side order of one of their perfectly cooked steaks for a real knockout meal.

There's also a RingSide East at 14021 NE Glisan St. (ℂ **503/ 255-0750**), on Portland's east side, with basically the same menu but not as much atmosphere; this one is open for lunch during the week.

2165 W. Burnside St. ℂ **503/223-1513.** www.ringsidesteakhouse.com. Reservations highly recommended. Steaks $14–$27; other main courses $15–$38. AE, DC, DISC, MC, V. Mon–Sat 5pm–midnight; Sun 4–11:30pm.

Wildwood ⟨★★⟩ NEW AMERICAN   With a menu that changes daily and a spare, elegant interior decor straight out of *Architectural Digest,* Wildwood has for many years been considered one of Portland's best restaurants. Lately, however, dishes have been a bit hit-or-miss, with the appetizers, salads, and desserts often outshining the entrees. But if you love creative cuisine you may still want to give this place a try. Fresh seasonal ingredients combined into simple-yet-imaginative dishes are the hallmark of chef Cory Schreiber's cooking, and often there are no more than four ingredients in a dish so as to let each of the flavors shine through. On a recent evening, there were skillet-roasted Washington mussels with garlic, tomato, and saffron and an excellent oyster-topped salad with pancetta and aïoli. This is the only non-Indian restaurant we know of that has a tandoor oven, and you can usually count on the meat dishes that are roasted in this oven. Salads and sorbets are exceptionally good. If you can't get a reservation, you can still usually get served at the bar.

1221 NW 21st Ave. ℂ **503/248-WOOD.** www.wildwoodrestaurant.citysearch. com. Reservations highly recommended. Main courses $9–$13 at lunch, $16–$25 at dinner. AE, MC, V. Mon–Sat 11:30am–2:30pm and 5:30–10pm; Sun 10am–2pm (brunch).

MODERATE

Caffe Mingo ⟨★★⟩ *(Finds)* ITALIAN   This intimate little neighborhood restaurant has terrific food, an interior as attractive as that of any other upscale restaurant here on Restaurant Row, and lower prices. If there's any problem with this immensely popular place it's that you almost always have to wait for a table and they only take reservations for larger parties. The solution? Get here as early as possible. The menu is short, and focuses on painstakingly prepared Italian comfort food. Just about all of the items on the menu are winners, from the antipasto platter, which might include roasted fennel, fresh mozzarella, and roasted red pepper, to an unusual penne pasta dish with tender beef braised in Chianti and espresso. The *panna cotta* dessert ("cooked cream" with fruit) is reason enough to come back here again and again, even if you have to wait in the rain to get a seat.

807 NW 21st Ave. ✆ 503/226-4646. Reservations accepted only for parties of 6 or more. Main courses $8.50–$18. AE, DISC, MC, V. Sun–Thurs 5–10pm; Fri–Sat 5–11pm.

Fratelli 🐾🐾 REGIONAL ITALIAN In this rustic-yet-chic restaurant, cement walls provide a striking contrast to dramatic draperies and candles that drip casually onto the tabletops. Dishes are consistently good, with surprisingly moderate prices for the Pearl District. There's excellent olive oil to go with your bread and an *antipasto* plate that's far more creative than your usual platter of meat, cheese, and pickled vegetables. On a recent visit, everything we tasted, from spring beans with arugula and octopus to chicken wrapped in prosciutto to rabbit *crepinette* (a sort of sausage) to a luscious panna cotta, was thoroughly satisfying. This restaurant's aesthetic and menu are similar to Caffe Mingo's (see above), but at Fratelli you can make reservations.

1230 NW Hoyt St. ✆ 503/241-8800. Reservations recommended. Main courses $11–$16.50. AE, DC, MC, V. Sun–Thurs 5:30–9pm; Fri–Sat 5:30–10pm.

Tapeo 🐾🐾 *(Finds)* SPANISH This a great place for a light meal or a romantic evening out. With the feeling of an old European restaurant, this small yet plush neighborhood spot nestled deep in Northwest Portland seems intimate, but the noise level rises considerably when the place is full—which is often. People wait around for the tables, which are placed so close together that you might as well be sitting with your neighbor. But it's worth the wait for authentic Spanish tapas such as excellent grilled eggplant thinly sliced and stuffed with goat cheese and deliciously crisp fried calamari served with aïoli. The flan is the richest you'll ever taste. Prices on wines, both by the glass and bottle, are decent.

2764 NW Thurman St. ✆ **503/226-0409.** Reservations not accepted. Tapas
$1.75–$9. DISC, MC, V. Tues–Thurs 5:30–10pm; Fri–Sat 5–10:30pm.

Typhoon! ✦ THAI   Located just off NW 23rd Avenue, this
trendy spot is a bit pricey for a Thai restaurant, but the unusual
menu offerings generally aren't available at other Portland Thai
restaurants. Be sure to start a meal with the *miang kum,* which con-
sists of dried shrimp, tiny chilies, ginger, lime, peanuts, shallots, and
toasted coconut drizzled with a sweet-and-sour sauce and wrapped
up in a spinach leaf. The burst of flavors on your taste buds is
absolutely astounding. (We first had this in Thailand and waited
years to get it in the United States.) The whole front wall of the
restaurant slides away for Thai-style open-air dining in the summer.
There is an extensive tea list.

There's another **Typhoon!** at 400 SW Broadway (✆ **503/
224-8285**), in the Imperial Hotel.

2310 NW Everett St. ✆ **503/243-7557.** Reservations recommended. Main courses
$7–$20. AE, DC, DISC, MC, V. Mon–Fri 11:30am–2:30pm; Sat noon–3pm;
Mon–Thurs 5–9:30pm; Fri–Sat 5–10:30pm; Sun 4:30–9:30pm.

INEXPENSIVE

Garbonzo's MIDDLE EASTERN/LATE-NIGHT DINING
This casual little place calls itself a falafel bar and is a popular spot
for a late-night meal (but it's also good for lunch or dinner). The
menu includes all the usual Middle Eastern offerings, most of which
also happen to be American Heart Association approved. You can
eat at one of the tiny cafe tables or get your order to go. They even
serve beer and wine.

Other Garbonzo's are at 3433 SE Hawthorne Blvd. (✆ **503/
239-6087**) and 6341 SW Capitol Hwy. (✆ **503/293-7335**).

922 NW 21st Ave. ✆ **503/227-4196.** Sandwiches $4–$5; dinners $7–$9. AE, DISC,
MC, V. Sun–Thurs 11:30am–12:30am; Fri–Sat 11:30am–2am (closed 1 hr. earlier
Oct–June).

Ken's Home Plate ✦ *Finds* INTERNATIONAL   You could easily overlook this little hole-in-the-wall, but once you step inside and
see the beautifully prepared foods in the display cases, you'll probably be as hooked as we are. Eating here once is enough to have you
dreaming about living in the neighborhood, so you could get all
your meals here. Chef/owner Ken Gordon turns out dishes that
would do justice to the best restaurants in town, and on any given
day 15 to 20 different entrees such as salmon strudel, Tuscan meat-
loaf, chicken Marsala, and Louisiana gumbo are available. However,

you might have trouble getting past the delicious sandwiches, which come with a side of any of more than half a dozen salads. Desserts are prominently displayed on the countertop, making them very difficult to ignore. Although this is primarily a takeout place, there are a few tables in case you can't wait to dig in.

1208 NW Glisan St. ⓒ 503/517-8935. Plates and sandwiches $5–$8.50. MC, V. Tues–Sat 11am–8pm; until 9pm 1st Thurs of each month.

Kornblatts DELICATESSEN   In the heart of NW 23rd Avenue, a dozen tables and a takeout corner are the setting for some very satisfying (and kosher) Jewish soul food. The corned beef and pastrami come directly from New York, and the bagels are made on the premises. If Nova lox, whitefish salad, knishes, potato latkes, or blintzes don't tempt you, how about a selection of five different kinds of cheesecake?

628 NW 23rd Ave. ⓒ 503/242-0055. Reservations not accepted. Sandwiches $5–$10. AE, MC, V. Mon–Fri 7am–8pm; Sat–Sun 7:30am–9pm.

Swagat ⓐ ⓥⁿˡᵘᵉ INDIAN   Located on the same corner as Garbonzo's (see above) is an exceptionally good Indian restaurant specializing in south Indian dishes. The *dosas,* crepes made of lentil flour stuffed with vegetable curry and served with a variety of sauces, are deliciously savory, and the tandoori chicken is intriguingly smoky. Be sure to start your meal with the sambar, a thin but flavorful soup. We also like the vegetable samosas, crisp turnovers stuffed with potatoes and peas, and the *keema mattar* (ground lamb with peas). Don't forget to order some of the puffy nan. At lunch, there is an extensive buffet that at $6.95 is a very good deal.

Another Swagat is located in the west-side suburb of Beaverton at 4325 SW 109th Ave. (ⓒ 503/626-3000).

2074 NW Lovejoy St. ⓒ 503/227-4300. Reservations not accepted. Main courses $7–$14. AE, DISC, MC, V. Daily 11:30am–2:30pm and 5–10pm.

3 Southwest Portland

EXPENSIVE

Chart House ⓐⓐ SEAFOOD   Although this place is a part of a national restaurant chain with lots of outposts all over California and the rest of the West, it also happens to boast the best view of any restaurant in Portland. On top of that, it serves the best New England clam chowder in the state. (The recipe repeatedly won awards in a Boston chowder competition.) While you savor your chowder, you can marvel at the views of the Willamette River,

Mount Hood, Mount St. Helens, and nearly all of Portland's east side. Fresh fish, either grilled, baked, or blackened is the house specialty. You'll also find a selection of excellent steaks for the problem child in your group who just won't eat seafood. No dinner here is complete without the hot chocolate lava cake, which has to be ordered at the start of your meal if you want it to be ready when you are.

The Chart House is in an out-of-the-way spot about a 10-minute drive from downtown Portland; be sure to call ahead and get driving directions.

5700 SW Terwilliger Blvd. ℭ 503/246-6963. Reservations recommended. Main courses $10–$16 at lunch, $15–$40 at dinner. AE, DC, DISC, MC, V. Mon–Fri 11:30am–2pm; Mon–Sat 5–10pm; Sun 5–9pm.

INEXPENSIVE

For Middle Eastern fare, there's a branch of **Garbonzo's** at 6341 SW Capitol Hwy. (ℭ **503/293-7335**). See the complete review on p. 69.

There's also a **Chez José West** at 8502 SW Terwilliger Blvd. (ℭ **503/244-0007**); see the review of Chez José East on p. 73.

The Old Spaghetti Factory ℛ ⟨Kids⟩ ITALIAN   Sure, this is a chain restaurant, but incredibly low prices, great decor, a waterfront location on the bank of the Willamette River, and the fact that the chain was born right here in Portland are reason enough to give this place a chance. This is the best waterfront restaurant in town for kids, and it's a lot of fun for grown-ups, too. Sort of a cross between a church, a trolley depot, and a Victorian brothel, this restaurant will keep you entertained and won't cost much more than McDonald's. Although this place is less than a mile from downtown, you should call for directions, then, as you're driving, watch for the big building with the blue tile roof.

0715 SW Bancroft St. ℭ 503/222-5375. www.osf.com. Reservations accepted only for large parties. Main courses $5.75–$9.25. AE, DISC, MC, V. Mon–Thurs 11:30am–2pm and 5–10pm, Fri 11:30am–2pm and 5–11pm, Sat 11:30am–11pm, Sun 11:30am–10pm; Memorial Day–Labor Day Mon–Fri 11:30am–10pm, Sat 11:30am–11pm, Sun 11:30am–10pm.

4 Northeast Portland (Including Irvington)

MODERATE

Rustica Italian Caffe ℛ ⟨Kids⟩ ITALIAN   If you're looking for good, moderately priced Italian food in Northeast Portland, look no further than Rustica. The menu is long, portions are large, and they

(Kids) Family-Friendly Restaurants

Aztec Willie & Joey Rose Tacqueria (*see below*)   Cheap Mexican and a glassed-in children's play area make this a good choice for families on a budget.

Chez José East (*p. 73*)   Kids under 6 eat free at this friendly Mexican restaurant between 5 and 7pm.

Newport Bay Restaurant (*p. 63*)   A cheery atmosphere, straightforward meals, and a great location on the Willamette River make this a good family pick.

The Old Spaghetti Factory (*p. 71*)   The inexpensive food, waterfront location, and eclectic decor are a hit with kids and parents alike.

Old Wives' Tales (*p. 76*)   This is just about the best place in Portland to eat if you've got small children. There are children's menus at all meals, and in the back of the restaurant there's a playroom that will keep your kids entertained while you enjoy your meal.

Rustica Italian Caffe (*p. 71*)   A long menu of kiddie-friendly food and an unpretentious atmosphere.

have a nice selection of Chiantis and great bread. What more could you ask for? In addition, the atmosphere is unpretentious, the space light and airy, and it's a popular spot for families. There is also a small pizzeria adjacent to the main restaurant. Among our favorite dishes here are the smoked-salmon cannelloni and the prawns sautéed in olive oil with grapefruit, rosemary, chili flakes, and cream.

1700 NE Broadway. ℂ **503/288-0990.** Reservations recommended. Main courses $11–$17. AE, DISC, MC, V. Mon–Fri 11:30am–2:30pm; Mon–Thurs 5–9:30pm; Fri–Sat 5–10:30pm; Sun 5–9pm.

INEXPENSIVE

Aztec Willie & Joey Rose Tacqueria *(Kids* MEXICAN   It's hard to miss this hip-yet-casual Mexican place with its copper pyramid over the front door and Mayan glyphs decorating the facade. Associated with perennial favorite Mayas Tacqueria in downtown Portland, Aztec Willie is a big place where you order cafeteria-style. For adults, there's a bar, and for kids, there's a glassed-in play area.

1501 NE Broadway. (C) **503/280-8900.** Reservations not accepted. Main courses $3–$9. AE, DISC, MC, V. Daily 11am–11pm.

Chez José East 👤 *Kids* MEXICAN   It's obvious both from the hip decor and the menu that this isn't Taco Bell. Although a squash enchilada with peanut sauce (spicy and sweet with mushrooms, apples, jicama, and sunflower seeds) sounds weird, it actually tastes great. Don't worry, though, there's also plenty of traditional—and traditionally cheap—fare on the menu. Because the restaurant doesn't take reservations, it's a good idea to get here early, before the line starts snaking out the door. This is a family-friendly place, so don't hesitate to bring the kids, and if the kids are under 6, they'll eat for free between 5 and 7pm.

2200 NE Broadway. (C) **503/280-9888.** Reservations accepted for 7 or more. Main courses $5.75–$11.50. AE, MC, V. Mon–Thurs 11:30am–11pm; Fri–Sat 11:30am–midnight; Sun 5–10pm.

Pizza Schmizza 👤 PIZZA   With creative pizzas and wacky decor, Pizza Schmizza is a great place to grab a slice or an entire pie. Of course there are old favorites such as cheese and pepperoni, but there are also such pizzas as spicy Thai and Yucatán-style, and several that have spaghetti as well as other ingredients on them. You can go Northwest and get a smoked salmon pizza, or try a Cajun pizza with alligator meat.

1422 NE Broadway (C) **503/517-9981.** www.schmizza.com. Pizzas $12–$28. AE, DISC, MC, V. Mon–Thurs 11am–10pm; Fri–Sat 11am–11pm; Sun noon–9pm.

5 Hawthorne, Belmont & Inner Southeast Portland

VERY EXPENSIVE

Genoa 👤👤👤 REGIONAL ITALIAN   This has long been the best Italian restaurant in Portland, and with fewer than a dozen tables, it's also one of the smallest. Everything, from the breads to the luscious desserts, is made fresh in the kitchen with the best local seasonal ingredients. This is an ideal setting for a romantic dinner, and service is attentive—the waiter explains dishes in detail as they are served, and dishes are magically whisked away as they're finished. The fixed-price menu changes every couple of weeks, but a typical dinner might start with *bagna cauda,* a creamy garlic and anchovy fondue, followed by spicy mussel soup. The pasta course could be a lasagna, with braised fresh artichokes layered with a béchamel sauce and Parmigiano-Reggiano cheese. There's always a choice of main courses, such as trout stuffed with chanterelle mushrooms, prosciutto, and tomatoes or pan-roasted rabbit with fennel and white wine. It takes Herculean restraint to choose from a selection that includes chocolate and nut tortes, fresh berry tarts, or liqueur-infused desserts.

2832 SE Belmont St. ℂ **503/238-1464.** www.genoarestaurant.com. Reservations required. Fixed-price 4-course dinner $56, 7-course dinner $68. AE, DC, DISC, MC, V. Mon–Sat 5:30–9:30pm (4-course dinner limited to 5:30 and 6pm seatings only).

EXPENSIVE

Castagna 🕭🕭 FRENCH/ITALIAN   Located on a rather nondescript stretch of Hawthorne Boulevard and much removed from the bustle of this boulevard's central commercial area, Castagna is a magnet for Portland foodies. Considering the less than stylish setting and minimalist (though thoroughly designed) interior, it's obvious that the food's the thing here. Dishes tend toward simple preparations that allow the freshness of the ingredients to express themselves. A friend swears the New York steak, served with a heaping mound of shoestring potatoes, is the best he's ever had; no wonder it's a house favorite here. However, less familiar entrees, such as salmon with fingerling potatoes and preserved Meyer lemon salsa or grilled rack of lamb with mint salsa verde and fava-bean salad, flesh out the menu. In addition to the main dining room, there is a more casual and inexpensive cafe dining room serving much simpler fare.

1752 SE Hawthorne Blvd. ℂ **503/231-7373.** Reservations highly recommended. Main dishes $20–$28; cafe main courses $9–$18. AE, DC, DISC, MC, V. Tues–Thurs 6–10pm; Fri 6–10:30pm; Sat 5:30–10:30pm.

MODERATE

Assaggio 🕭🕭 RUSTIC ITALIAN   This trattoria in the Sellwood neighborhood focuses on pastas and wines; the menu lists 15 pastas, and the wine list includes more than 100 wines, almost all Italian. The atmosphere in this tiny place is theatrical, with indirect lighting, dark walls, and the likes of Mario Lanza playing in the background. The pastas, with surprisingly robust flavors, are the main attraction. Don't be surprised if after taking your first bite, you suddenly hear a Verdi aria. *Assaggio* means a sampling or a taste, and that is exactly what you get if you order salad, bruschetta, or pasta Assaggio-style—a sampling of several dishes, all served family-style. This is especially fun if you're here with a group.

7742 SE 13th Ave. ℂ **503/232-6151.** www.assaggiorestaurant.com. Reservations accepted (and recommended) only Tues–Thurs or for parties of 6 or more. Main courses $10–$16. MC, V. Tues–Thurs 5–9:30pm; Fri–Sat 5–10pm.

INEXPENSIVE

For Middle Eastern fare, there's a branch of **Garbonzo's** at 3433 SE Hawthorne Blvd. (✆ **503/239-6087**). See the complete review on p. 69.

Chez Grill ✆ SOUTHWEST   Brought to you by the owners of Portland's popular Chez José restaurants, Chez Grill leans more toward nuevo Mexican or Southwestern flavors. Although the restaurant is at the western end of the Hawthorne district, it looks as if it could have been transported straight from Tucson or Santa Fe. Whatever you do, don't miss the grilled fish tacos; they're the best in town! The grilled prawn enchilada is also exquisite, although you only get one (with rice and beans). Be sure to start a meal with the rough-cut guacamole; for a strangely sweet appetizer, try the unusual stuffed avocado.

2229 SE Hawthorne Blvd. ✆ **503/239-4002.** www.chezgrill.citysearch.com. Main courses $6.25–$14. DISC, MC, V. Mon–Thurs 4–10pm; Fri–Sat 4–11pm; Sun 5–10pm (bar open later nightly).

Esparza's Tex-Mex Café ✆ *Finds* TEX-MEX   With red-eyed cow skulls on the walls and marionettes, model planes, and stuffed iguanas and armadillos hanging from the ceiling, the decor here can only be described as Tex-eclectic, a description that is just as appropriately applied to the menu. Sure there are enchiladas and tamales and tacos, but they might be filled with ostrich, buffalo meat, or smoked salmon. Rest assured Esparza's also serves standard ingredients such as chicken and beef. Main courses come with some pretty good rice and beans, and if you want your meal hotter, they'll toss you a couple of jalapeños. The *nopalitos* (fried cactus) are worth a try, and the margaritas just might be the best in Portland. While you're waiting for a seat (there's almost always a wait), check out the vintage tunes on the jukebox.

2725 SE Ankeny St. ✆ **503/234-7909.** Reservations not accepted. Main courses $7.25–$14.50. AE, DC, DISC, MC, V. Tues–Sat 11:30am–10pm (in summer Fri–Sat until 10:30pm).

Nicholas's *Finds* MIDDLE EASTERN   This little hole-in-the-wall on an unattractive stretch of Grand Avenue is usually packed at mealtimes, and it's not the decor or ambience that pulls people in. The big draw is the great food and cheap prices. In spite of the heat from the pizza oven and the crowded conditions, the customers and wait staff still manage to be friendly. Our favorite dish is the *Manakish,* Mediterranean pizza with thyme, oregano, sesame seeds, olive oil, and lemony-flavored sumac. Also available are a creamy hummus, baba ghanouj, kebabs, falafel, and gyros.

318 SE Grand Ave. (between Pine and Oak sts.). ✆ **503/235-5123.** Reservations not accepted. Main courses $4.25–$10.75. No credit cards. Mon–Sat 11am–9pm; Sun noon–9pm.

Old Wives' Tales 🌿 (Kids) INTERNATIONAL/VEGETARIAN Old Wives' Tales is a Portland countercultural institution. The menu is mostly vegetarian, with multi-ethnic dishes such as spanakopita and burritos and a smattering of chicken and seafood dishes. Breakfasts here are excellent and are served until 2pm daily. Old Wives' Tales's other claim to fame these days is as the city's best place to eat out with kids. The restaurant has plenty of meal choices for children, and there's a big playroom where the kids can stay busy while you enjoy your meal.

1300 E Burnside St. ✆ **503/238-0470.** Reservations recommended for parties of 5 or more. Breakfasts $5–$7; lunch and dinner main courses $6–$13. AE, DC, DISC, MC, V. Sun–Thurs 8am–9pm; Fri–Sat 8am–10pm.

6 Westmoreland & Sellwood

EXPENSIVE

Caprial's Bistro and Wine 🌿🌿 NORTHWEST If you're a foodie, you're probably already familiar with celebrity chef Caprial Pence, who helped put the Northwest on the national restaurant map and has since gone on to write several cookbooks and host TV and radio food shows. That her eponymously named restaurant is a fairly casual place tucked away in a quiet residential neighborhood in Southeast Portland may come as a surprise. The menu changes monthly and is limited to four or five main dishes and about twice as many appetizers. Entrees combine perfectly cooked meat and seafood with vibrant sauces such as cherry barbecue sauce. Pork loin is always a good bet here, as are the seasonal seafood dishes. Desserts are usually rich without being overly sweet. There is also a wine bar offering a superb selection of wines at reasonable prices.

7015 SE Milwaukie Ave. ✆ **503/236-6457.** Dinner reservations highly recommended. Main courses $7–$12 at lunch, $20–$26 at dinner. MC, V. Tues–Fri 11am–3pm; Sat 11:30am–3pm; Tues–Thurs 5–9pm; Fri–Sat 5–9:30pm.

MODERATE

Saburo's Sushi House 🌿🌿 JAPANESE This tiny sushi restaurant is so enormously popular that there is almost always a line out the door, and as people linger over their sushi, frequently ordering "just one more," the line doesn't always move very fast. But when you finally do get a seat and your sushi arrives, you'll know it was worth the wait. The big slabs of fresh fish drape over the sides of the little cubes of rice, leaving no question about whether you get your money's worth here. Our favorites are the *sabu* roll and the maguro tuna sushi, with generous slabs of tuna.

1667 SE Bybee Blvd. ℂ **503/236-4237.** Reservations not accepted. Main courses $8–$16; sushi $2.50–$7. DISC, MC, V. Mon–Thurs 5–9:30pm; Fri 5–10:30pm; Sat 4:30–10pm; Sun 4:30–9pm.

INEXPENSIVE

El Palenque *Finds* SALVADORAN/MEXICAN   Though El Palenque also bills itself as a Mexican restaurant, the Salvadoran dishes are the real reason to come. If you've never had a *pupusa,* this is your chance; it's basically an extra thick corn tortilla with a meat or cheese filling, accompanied by spicy shredded cabbage. Instead of adding the filling after the tortilla is cooked, the filling goes in beforehand, so you end up with a sort of griddle-cooked turnover. Accompany your pupusa with some fried plantains and a glass of *horchata* (sweet and spicy rice drink) for a typical Salvadoran meal.

8324 SE 17th Ave. ℂ **503/231-5140.** Main courses $5–$13. AE, MC, V. Daily 11:30am–9:30pm.

7 Coffee, Tea, Bakeries & Pastry Shops

CAFES

If you'd like to sample some cafes around Portland that serve not only the full range of coffee drinks, but are also atmospheric, we recommend the following:

Café Lena, 2239 SE Hawthorne Blvd. (ℂ **503/238-7087**), located in the funky Hawthorne District, has occasional live music and tasty food but is best known for its poetry nights.

Located out beyond Hawthorne Boulevard's main shopping district, **Common Grounds,** 4321 SE Hawthorne Blvd. (ℂ **503/236-4835**), is a countercultural hangout where the magazine rack is filled with literary reviews, small press journals, and other lefty literature. The crowd of coffee drinkers tends to be tattooed and pierced.

Peet's Coffee *, 508 SW Broadway (ℂ **503/973-5540**), a relative newcomer in Portland, is notable not only for its great (and strong) coffee, but also for the fact that the space here is much larger than at any Peet's you'd find in Berkeley, California, where the chain originated.

Torrefazione Italia ☆☆, 838 NW 23rd Ave. (© **503/ 228-1255**), serves its classic brew in hand-painted Italian crockery and has a good selection of pastries to go with your drink. Order a latte just to see what a wonderful job they do with the foam. Other locations are at 1403 NE Weidler (© **503/288-1608**) and 1140 NW Everett (© **503/224-9896**).

BAKERIES & PASTRY SHOPS

Pearl Bakery ☆☆, 102 NW Ninth Ave. (© **503/827-0910**), in the heart of the SoHo-like Pearl district, is famous for its breads and European-style pastries. The gleaming bakery cafe is also good for sandwiches, such as the roasted eggplant and tomato pesto on crusty bread.

The **Rimsky-Korsakoffee House** ☆, 707 SE 12th Ave. (© **503/ 232-2640**), a classic old-style coffeehouse (complete with mismatched chairs), has been Portland's favorite dessert hangout for more than a decade. Live classical music and great desserts keep patrons loyal. (The mocha fudge cake is small but deadly.) There's no sign on the old house, but you'll know this is the place as soon as you open the door. Open after 7pm and until midnight on weekdays, 1am on weekends.

Say the words *Papa Haydn* to a Portlander, and you'll see a blissful smile appear. What is it about this little bistro that sends locals into accolades of superlatives? The desserts. The lemon chiffon torte, raspberry gâteau, black velvet, and tiramisu at **Papa Haydn West** ☆☆, 701 NW 23rd Ave. (© **503/228-7317**), are legendary. There's another location at 5829 SE Milwaukie Ave. (© **503/ 232-9440**) in Sellwood.

Located in Ladd's Addition, an old neighborhood full of big trees and craftsman-style bungalows, **Palio Dessert House** ☆, 1996 SE Ladd Ave. (© **503/232-9412**), is a very relaxed place with a timeless European quality. Hang out, play chess, or listen to music while you enjoy a slice of Key lime pie or banana bread. To get there, take Hawthorne Boulevard east to the corner of 12th and Hawthorne, then go diagonally down Ladd Avenue.

8 Quick Bites & Cheap Eats

If you're just looking for something quick, cheap, and good to eat, there are lots of great options around the city. Downtown, at **Good Dog/Bad Dog,** 708 SW Alder St. (© **503/222-3410**), you'll find handmade sausages. The bratwurst with kraut and onions is a good deal.

Designer pizzas topped with anything from roasted eggplant to wild mushrooms to Thai peanut sauce can be had at **Pizzicato Gourmet Pizza** 𝄐. Find them downtown at 705 SW Alder St. (© **503/226-1007**); in Northwest at 505 NW 23rd Ave. (© **503/242-0023**); and in Southeast at 2811 E. Burnside (© **503/236-6045**).

In the Pearl District, there's **In Good Taste** 𝄐 at 231 NW 11th Ave. (© **503/241-7960**), a cooking school and store that also serves a bistro lunch. Order such items as caramelized tomato tart and maple-spice pork loin sandwich at the counter and grab a seat.

Over in Southeast Portland, you can't miss the **Kitchen Table Café,** 400 SE 12th Ave. (© **503/230-6977**), in the yellow and purple building on the corner of SE Oak and SE 12th streets. This is a great place for homemade soups, salads, and sandwiches.

If you're in the mood for a picnic, **Elephant's Delicatessen,** 13 NW 23rd Place (© **503/224-3955**), is a good place to go for your supplies, including cheeses, sandwiches, wines, and yummy desserts. Head up to nearby Washington Park to enjoy it all.

If you find your energy flagging while shopping in the funky Hawthorne district, do as the French do and a grab a filling little crepe. **Chez Machin,** 3553 SE Hawthorne Blvd. (© **503/736-9381**), can whip up any of more than two dozen sweet or savory crepes for you. If you've got a sweet tooth, be sure to try the Nutella custard crepe. This place also operates a crepe cart on NW 23rd Avenue.

6

Exploring Portland

Most American cities boast about their museums and historic buildings, shopping, and restaurants; Portland, as always, is different. Ask a Portlander about the city's must-see attractions, and you'll probably be directed to the Japanese Garden, the International Rose Test Garden, and the Portland Saturday Market.

This isn't to say that the Portland Art Museum, which specializes in blockbuster exhibits, isn't worth visiting or that there are no historic buildings around. It's just that Portland's gardens, thanks to the weather here, are some of the finest in the country. What's more, all the rainy weather seems to keep artists indoors creating beautiful art and crafts for much of the year, work that many artists sell at the Portland Saturday Market.

Gardening is a Portland obsession, and there are numerous world-class public gardens and parks within the city. Visiting all the city's gardens alone can take up 2 or 3 days of touring, so leave plenty of time in your schedule if you have a green thumb.

Once you've seen the big attractions, it's time to start learning why everyone loves living here so much. Portlanders for the most part are active types, who enjoy snow-skiing on Mount Hood and hiking in the Columbia Gorge just as much as going to art museums. So no visit to Portland would be complete without venturing out into the Oregon countryside. Within 1½ hours you can be skiing on Mount Hood, walking beside the chilly waters of the Pacific, sampling Pinot Noir in wine country, or hiking beside a waterfall in the Columbia Gorge. However, for those who prefer urban activities, the museums and parks listed below should satisfy.

SUGGESTED ITINERARIES

If You Have 1 Day

Start your day in Washington Park at the **Rose Garden** (the roses are in bloom June–Sept) and the **Japanese Garden** (lovely any time of year). After touring these two gardens, head downhill into downtown Portland. If you can make it to **Pioneer Courthouse**

Square by noon, you can catch the day's weather prediction on the *Weather Machine* sculpture. From here, head over to the South Parks Blocks and visit the **Portland Art Museum,** which usually has some big show going on. Across the park from this museum is the **Oregon History Center,** where you can finish your day. If it's the weekend, be sure to squeeze in time to visit the **Saturday Market** (open both Sat and Sun; closed Jan–Feb), in the Skidmore Historic District.

If You Have 2 Days

Follow the outline above for your first day in town. On your second day, head up the **Columbia Gorge** to see its many beautiful waterfalls. If you get an early start, you can loop all the way around **Mount Hood** and maybe get in a little hiking from historic Timberline Lodge.

If You Have 3 Days

Follow the 2-day strategy as outlined above. On your third day, explore some of the historic blocks in the **Old Town** neighborhood (take in the Sat Market if you haven't already), and perhaps visit the **Oregon Maritime Center and Museum.** Then walk through **Tom McCall Waterfront Park,** at the south end of which you can catch a historic trolley that runs to the posh suburb of **Lake Oswego.** Alternatively, you could take a scenic **cruise** on the river or do some paddling on a guided **sea kayak tour** on the Willamette.

If You Have 4 Days or More

Follow the 3-day strategy as outlined above. On Day 4, head over to the beach; it's only about 1½ hours away. You can stroll around artsy **Cannon Beach** and explore nearby **Ecola State Park.** Then make your way down the coast, stopping at other small state parks along the way. You can head back to Portland from **Tillamook.** If you have time, do part or all of the **Three Capes Scenic Loop** outside of Tillamook before returning to Portland.

On Day 5, venture north to **Mount St. Helens** for the day to see the devastation that was caused when this volcano erupted back in 1980. Along the way, you could stop and visit historic Fort Vancouver in **Vancouver, Washington.** If you're a wine fancier, skip Mount St. Helens and instead head west from Portland for some **wine tasting.**

1 Downtown Portland's Cultural District

Any visit to Portland should start at the corner of Southwest Broadway and Yamhill Street on **Pioneer Courthouse Square.** The

Portland Attractions

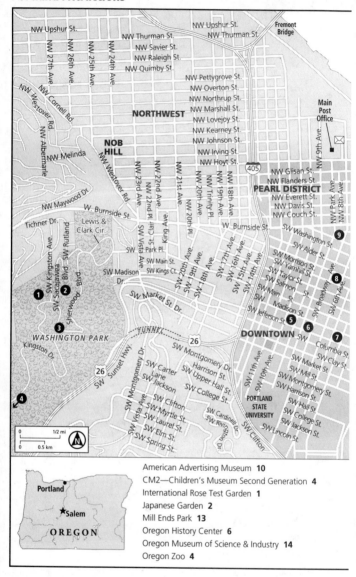

American Advertising Museum **10**
CM2—Children's Museum Second Generation **4**
International Rose Test Garden **1**
Japanese Garden **2**
Mill Ends Park **13**
Oregon History Center **6**
Oregon Museum of Science & Industry **14**
Oregon Zoo **4**

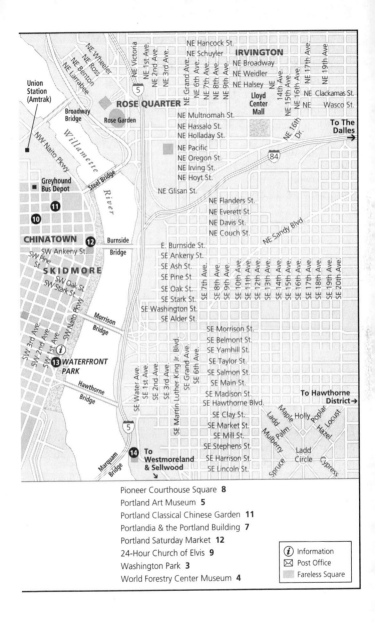

Pioneer Courthouse Square **8**

Portland Art Museum **5**

Portland Classical Chinese Garden **11**

Portlandia & the Portland Building **7**

Portland Saturday Market **12**

24-Hour Church of Elvis **9**

Washington Park **3**

World Forestry Center Museum **4**

(i) Information
⊠ Post Office
▢ Fareless Square

83

brick-paved square is an outdoor stage for everything from flower displays to concerts to protest rallies, but not too many years ago this beautiful area was nothing but a parking lot. The parking lot was created in 1951 when the Portland Hotel, an architectural gem of a Queen Anne–style château, was controversially razed to the ground.

Today the square, with its tumbling waterfall fountain and free-standing columns, is Portland's favorite gathering spot, especially at noon, when the *Weather Machine* ⟨*⟩, a mechanical sculpture, forecasts the weather for the next 24 hours. Amid a fanfare of music and flashing lights, the Weather Machine sends up clouds of mist and then either a sun (clear weather), a dragon (stormy weather), or a blue heron (clouds and drizzle) appears.

Keep your eyes on the square's brick pavement, too. Every brick contains a name (or names) or statement, and some are rather curious. Also on the square, you'll find the **Portland Oregon Visitor Association Information Center,** a Starbucks espresso bar, and Powell's Travel Store. Unfortunately, you'll also find plenty of street kids hanging out here all hours of the day and night, so don't be surprised if they ask you for spare change.

Also not to be missed in this neighborhood are *Portlandia* ⟨*⟩⟨*⟩ and the **Portland Building,** 1120 SW Fifth Ave. Symbol of the city, *Portlandia* is the second-largest hammered bronze statue in the country, second only to the Statue of Liberty. The massive kneeling figure holds a trident in one hand and reaches toward the street with the other. This classically designed figure perches incongruously above the entrance to the controversial Portland Building, considered to be the first postmodern structure in the country. Today anyone familiar with the bizarre constructions of Los Angeles architect Frank Gehry would find it difficult to understand how such an innocuous and attractive building could have ever raised such a fuss, but it did just that in the early '80s.

Oregon History Center ⟨*⟩ In the middle of the 19th century, the Oregon Territory was a land of promise and plenty. Thousands of hardy individuals set out along the Oregon Trail, crossing a vast and rugged country to reach the fertile valleys of this region. Others came by ship around the Horn. Those who wish to learn about the people who came to Oregon before them will enjoy this well-designed museum.

Fascinating educational exhibits chronicle Oregon's history from before the arrival of the first Europeans to well into the 20th century. The displays incorporate Native-American artifacts, a covered wagon, nautical and surveying instruments, and contemporary objects. Museum docents, with roots stretching back to the days of the Oregon Trail, are often on hand to answer questions. There's also a research library that includes many journals written by early pioneers. You can't miss this complex—look for the eight-story-high trompe l'oeil mural stretching across the front.

1200 SW Park Ave. ✆ **503/222-1741**. www.ohs.org. Admission $6 adults and seniors, $3 students, $1.50 children 6–12, free for children under 6, free for seniors on Thurs. Tues–Sat 10am–5pm (Thurs until 8pm); Sun noon–5pm. Bus: 6. MAX: Library Station. Portland Streetcar: Art Museum (northbound); 11th Ave. and Jefferson St. (southbound).

Portland Art Museum ⚘⚘   Although this relatively small art museum has a respectable collection of European, Asian, and American art, the museum has in recent years been positioning itself as the Northwest stop for touring blockbuster exhibits. Scheduled from June 1 to September 22, 2002, is "Splendors of Imperial Japan (Arts of the Meiji Period from the Khalili Collection)"; and from August 17 to December 1, 2002, the museum will be showing "Grandma Moses in the 21st Century." An expansion a couple of years ago added several new galleries and a small sculpture court to the museum. The galleries of Native-American art and Northwest art are now the museum's most impressive displays. October through May, on Wednesday nights, the Museum After Hours program presents live music. The adjacent **Northwest Film Center** is affiliated with the Art Museum and shows an eclectic mix of films.

1219 SW Park Ave. ✆ **503/226-2811**. www.portlandartmuseum.org. Admission $7.50 adults, $6 seniors and students, $4 children 5–18, free for children under 5. Tues–Sat 10am–5pm (Oct–May Wed 10am–8pm); Sun noon–5pm; first Thurs of each month until 8pm. Bus: 6. MAX: Library Station. Portland Streetcar: Art Museum (northbound); 11th Ave. and Jefferson St. (southbound).

2 Skidmore Historic District, Chinatown & the Willamette River Waterfront

If Pioneer Courthouse Square is the city's living room, **Tom McCall Waterfront Park** ⚘, along the Willamette River, is the city's party room and backyard play area. There are acres of lawns, shade trees, sculptures, and fountains, and the paved path through the park is popular with in-line skaters and joggers. This park also serves as the site of numerous festivals each summer. Also in the park are the Waterfront Story Garden, dedicated to storytellers, and the

Japanese-American Historical Plaza, dedicated to Japanese Americans who were sent to internment camps during World War II.

Just north of this plaza, a pedestrian walkway crosses the Steel Bridge to the east side of the Willamette River and the new **Eastside Promenade,** which stretches for about 1½ miles along the east bank of the river. Although this paved multi-use path gets a lot of traffic noise from the adjacent freeway, it offers great views of the Portland skyline. Along the route there are small parks and gardens, interesting sculptures, and benches for sitting and soaking up the view. The highlight of this path is a section that floats right on the river and is attached to pilings in much the same way that a floating dock is constructed. You can access the Eastside Promenade by way of the pedestrian pathway on the Steel Bridge. This bridge is at the north end of Waterfront Park.

Oregon Maritime Center and Museum Inside this museum you'll find models of ships that once plied the Columbia and Willamette. Also on display are early navigation instruments, artifacts from the battleship *Oregon,* old ship hardware, and other maritime memorabilia. The historic steam-powered sternwheeler *Portland,* moored across Waterfront Park from the museum, is also open to the public. Inside this old steam-powered paddle-wheel tugboat there are more displays about maritime history, and docents are on hand to answer questions about the boat itself.

113 SW Naito Pkwy. ⓒ **503/224-7724.** Admission $4 adults, $3 seniors, $2 children 8 and older, free for children under 8. Fri–Sun 11am–4pm (sometimes also open Wed–Thurs in summer). Bus: 12, 19, 20. MAX: Skidmore Fountain Station.

Oregon Museum of Science and Industry (OMSI) ⓖ *Kids* Located on the east bank of the Willamette River across from the south end of Waterfront Park, this modern science museum has six huge halls, and both kids and adults find the exhibits fun and fascinating. This is a hands-on museum, and everyone is urged to get involved with displays, from a discovery space for toddlers to physics and chemistry labs for older children. Simulated earthquakes and tornadoes are perennial favorites. There's plenty of pure entertainment at an **OMNIMAX theater** and the **Murdock Sky Theater,** which features laser-light shows and astronomy presentations. The USS *Blueback* submarine (used in the film *The Hunt for Red October*) is docked here, and tours are given daily.

Between mid-June and late September, **Samtrak** (ⓒ **503/653-2380**), a small open-air train, runs between OMSI and Oaks

Park Amusement Center. OMSI is also the departure point for several different boat cruises up and down the Willamette River.

1945 SE Water Ave. ✆ 800/955-6674 or 503/797-4000. www.omsi.edu. Museum or OMNIMAX $7 adults, $5 seniors and children 4–13; $4 submarine tours, $4 planetarium shows, laser-light shows $4 matinee, $7 evening; discounted combination tickets available. Thurs 2pm until closing all tickets are 2-for-1. Mid-June to Labor Day daily 9:30am–7pm; Labor Day to mid-June Tues–Sun 9:30am–5:30pm. Closed Christmas. Bus: 63.

Portland Saturday Market ★★   The Portland Saturday Market (actually held on both Sat and Sun) is arguably the city's single most important and best-loved event. Don't miss it. For years the Northwest has attracted artists and craftspeople, and every Saturday and Sunday nearly 300 of them can be found selling their creations here. In addition to the dozens of crafts stalls, you'll find ethnic and unusual foods and lots of free entertainment. This is one of the best places in Portland to shop for one-of-a-kind gifts. The atmosphere is always cheerful and the crowds colorful. Located at the heart of the Skidmore District, Portland Saturday Market makes an excellent starting or finishing point for a walk around Portland's downtown historic neighborhood. On Sunday, on-street parking is free.

Underneath the west end of the Burnside Bridge between SW First Ave. and SW Naito Pkwy. ✆ 503/222-6072. www.portlandsaturdaymarket.com. Free admission. First weekend in Mar–Christmas Eve Sat 10am–5pm and Sun 11am–4:30pm. Bus: 12, 19, or 20. MAX: Skidmore Fountain Station.

3 Washington Park & Portland's West Hills

Portland is justly proud of its green spaces, and foremost among them are **Washington Park** and **Forest Park.**

Within Washington Park, you'll find the Japanese Garden and International Rose Test Garden, which are adjacent to one another on the more developed east side of the park (see the listings below). On the west side of the park (farther from the city center), you'll find not only the Hoyt Arboretum but also the Oregon Zoo, World Forestry Center, and CM2—Children's Museum 2nd Generation.

The 175-acre **Hoyt Arboretum** (✆ 503/228-8733) ★ is planted with 800 species of trees and shrubs from temperate regions around the world. The arboretum has 10 miles of hiking trails and is a great place for a quick hike. Between April and October, there are free 1-hour guided tours of the arboretum on Saturdays and Sundays at 2pm. At the south end of the arboretum, adjacent to the World Forestry Center and the Oregon Zoo, is the **Vietnam Veterans Living Memorial.** At the Visitor Center, 4000 SW Fairview

Boulevard (open daily 9am–3pm), you can pick up maps and guides to the arboretum. The arboretum can be reached either from the Oregon Zoo/World Forestry Center/CM2—Children's Museum 2nd Generation area or by following the arboretum signs from West Burnside Street.

To the north of Hoyt Arboretum is **Forest Park** ★★ (© 503/ **823-PLAY**), which, with nearly 5,000 acres of forest, is the largest forested city park in the United States. Within the park, there are more than 65 miles of trails and old fire roads for hiking, jogging, and mountain biking. More than 100 species of birds call this forest home, making it a great spot for urban bird-watching. Along the forest trails, you can see huge old trees and find quiet picnic spots tucked away in the woods. One of the most convenient park access points is at the top of NW Thurman Street (just keep heading uphill until the road dead-ends). However, if you park at the Hoyt Arboretum Visitor Center (see above) or the Audubon Society (see below), you can pick up a map of Forest Park and head out from either of these locations.

Adjacent to Forest Park, you'll also find the **Portland Audubon Society,** 5151 NW Cornell Rd. (© 503/292-9453), which has a couple of miles of hiking trails on its forested property. In keeping with its mission to promote enjoyment, understanding, and protection of the natural world, these nature trails are open to the public. You can also visit the Nature Center or Wildlife Care Center here. To find this facility from downtown Portland, first drive to NW 23rd Avenue, and then head uphill on NW Lovejoy Street, which becomes NW Cornell Road. (*Warning:* Car break-ins are commonplace at the parking area just down the road from the Audubon Society, so don't leave anything of value in your car.)

By car, the easiest route to the Washington Park attractions from downtown Portland is to take SW Jefferson Street west, turn right onto SW 18th Avenue, left on SW Salmon Street, right on SW King Street, and then left onto SW Park Place. Although this sounds confusing, you'll find most of the route well marked with "Scenic Drive" signs. Alternatively, you can drive west on West Burnside Street and watch for signs to the arboretum, or take the zoo exit off U.S. 26. All of these attractions can also be reached via Bus 63. You can also take the MAX line to the Washington Park Station, which is adjacent to the Oregon Zoo, World Forestry Center, CM2—Children's Museum 2nd Generation, and Hoyt Arboretum. From here, it is possible (in the summer months) to take a bus shuttle to the Japanese Garden and International Rose Test Garden. There's

Great Photo Ops

If you've seen a photo of Portland with conical snow-covered Mount Hood looming in the background and you want to snap a similar photo while you're in town, there are several places to try. Most popular are probably the terraces of the International Rose Test Garden and from behind the pavilion at the Japanese Garden. Another great view can be had from the grounds of the Pittock Mansion. All three of these places are described in detail elsewhere in this chapter.

One other view is located atop Council Crest, a hilltop park in Portland's West Hills. To reach this park, take the Sylvan exit off U.S. 26 west of downtown Portland, turn south and then east (left) on Humphrey Boulevard, and then follow the signs. Alternatively, you can follow SW Broadway south out of downtown Portland and follow the signs. This road winds through attractive hillside neighborhoods for a ways before reaching Council Crest.

also a miniature train that runs from the zoo to a station near the two public gardens. However, to ride this train, you must first pay zoo admission.

International Rose Test Garden ★★   Covering 4½ acres of hillside in the West Hills above downtown Portland, these are among the largest and oldest rose test gardens in the United States and are the only city-maintained test gardens to bestow awards on each year's best roses. The gardens were established in 1917 by the American Rose Society and are used as a testing ground for new varieties of roses. Though you will probably see some familiar roses in the Gold Medal Garden, most of the 400 varieties on display are new hybrids being tested before marketing. Among the roses in bloom from late spring to early winter, you'll find a separate garden of miniature roses. There's also a Shakespeare Garden that includes flowers mentioned in the Bard's works. After seeing these acres of roses, you'll understand why Portland is known as the City of Roses and why the Rose Festival in June is the city's biggest annual celebration. The small Rose Garden Store (© **503/227-7033**), is packed with rose-inspired products.

400 SW Kingston Ave., Washington Park. ℂ **503/823-3636.** Free admission (donations accepted). Daily dawn–dusk. Bus: 63.

Japanese Garden ⋆⋆⋆   Considered the finest example of a Japanese garden in North America, Portland's Japanese Garden is one of the city's most popular attractions. Don't miss it. Not only are there five different styles of Japanese gardens scattered over 5½ acres, but there's also a view of volcanic Mount Hood, which has a strong resemblance to Mount Fuji.

Although Japanese gardens are traditionally not designed with colorful floral displays in mind, this garden definitely has its seasonal highlights. In early spring there are the cherry trees, in midspring there are the azaleas, in late spring a huge wisteria bursts into bloom, and in early summer, huge Japanese irises color the banks of a pond. Among the gardens, there's a beautiful and very realistic waterfall.

This is a very tranquil spot and is even more peaceful on rainy days when the crowds stay away, so don't pass up a visit just because it's raining. Also, on the third Saturday of each of the summer months, there's a demonstration of the Japanese tea ceremony in the garden's teahouse. There are also many special events held here throughout the year (ikebana, bonsai, Japanese-inspired art, and so on).

611 Kingston Ave. (in Washington Park). ℂ **503/223-1321.** www.japanesegarden. com. Admission $6 adults, $4 seniors, $3.50 students, free for children under 6. Apr 1–Sept 30 Tues–Sun 10am–7pm, Mon noon–7pm; Oct 1–Mar 31 Tues–Sun 10am–4pm, Mon noon–4pm. Closed Thanksgiving, Christmas, and New Year's Day. Bus: 63. MAX: Washington Park Station (then, in summer months, take the shuttle bus or the Zoo Train).

Oregon Zoo ⋆ *Kids*   The Oregon Zoo has the largest breeding herd of elephants in captivity and is perhaps best known for its elephants. However, in recent years, the zoo has been adding new exhibits and branching out beyond the world of pachyderms. The Africa exhibit, which includes a very lifelike rain forest and a

---

All Aboard!
The **Washington Park and Zoo Railway** travels between the zoo and the International Rose Test and Japanese gardens. Tickets for the miniature railway are $2.75 for adults, $2 for seniors and children 3 to 11.

savanna populated by zebras, rhinos, giraffes, hippos, and other animals, is one of the most realistic habitats you'll ever see at a zoo. Equally impressive is the Alaskan tundra exhibit, with grizzly bears, wolves, and musk oxen. The Cascade Crest exhibit includes mountain goat habitat, and in the Steller Cove exhibit, you can watch the antics of Steller's sea lions and sea otters. Don't miss the bat house. At press time, there were plans to open a new Amazon Flooded Forest exhibit in late 2001.

In the summer, there are **outdoor concerts** in the zoo's amphitheater; admission prices vary.

4001 SW Canyon Rd., Washington Park. (*C*) **503/226-1561**. www.oregonzoo.org. Admission $7.50 adults, $6 seniors, $4.50 children 3–11, free for under 2, free 2nd Tues of each month from 1pm to closing. Apr 1–Sept 30 daily 9am–6pm; Oct 1–Mar 31 daily 9am–4pm. Bus: 63. MAX: Washington Park Station.

Pittock Mansion (*A*)   At nearly the highest point in the West Hills, 1,000 feet above sea level, stands the most impressive mansion in Portland. Once slated to be torn down to make way for new housing, this grand château, built by the founder of Portland's *Oregonian* newspaper, is fully restored and open to the public. Built in 1914 in a French Renaissance style, the mansion featured many innovations, including a built-in vacuum system and amazing multiple showerheads in the baths. Today it's furnished with 18th- and 19th-century antiques, much as it might have been at the time the Pittocks lived here. With an expansive view over the city to the Cascade Range, the lawns surrounding the mansion are great for picnics. You can also access Forest Park's Wildwood Trail from here.

3229 NW Pittock Dr. (*C*) **503/823-3624**. Admission $5.50 adults, $5 seniors, $3 children 6–18. Daily noon–4pm. Closed 3 days in late Nov, most major holidays, and the month of Jan.

World Forestry Center Museum (*A*)   Although Oregon depends less and less on the timber industry with each passing year, the World Forestry Center Museum is still busy educating visitors about the importance of our forest resources. Step inside the huge wooden main hall, and you come face to bark with a very large and very lifelike tree. Press a button at its base and it tells you the story of how trees live and grow. In other rooms you can see exhibits on forests of the world, old-growth trees, a petrified wood exhibit, and a rainforest exhibit developed by the Smithsonian Institution. There are also interesting temporary exhibits staged here throughout the year, from photographic exhibits to displays of the woodworker's art.

4033 SW Canyon Rd. ⒸⒸ **503/228-1367.** www.worldforestry.org. Admission $4.50 adults, $3.50 seniors and children under 6. Daily 10am–5pm (9am–5pm Memorial Day–Labor Day). Closed Christmas. Bus: 63. MAX: Washington Park Station.

4 Portland's Other Public Gardens

For Portland's two best-loved public gardens, the **International Rose Test Garden** and the **Japanese Garden,** see "Washington Park & Portland's West Hills," earlier in this chapter.

If roses are your passion, you'll also want to check out the **Peninsula Park Rose Garden** at the corner of N. Portland Boulevard and N. Albina Avenue (take the Portland Blvd. exit off I-5 and go 2 blocks east), which has even more rose bushes than the International Rose Test Garden.

The Berry Botanic Garden ⚐   Originally founded as a private garden, the Berry Botanic Garden is now one of Portland's favorite public gardens. Among the highlights is a large, forestlike collection of mature rhododendron shrubs. There are also a native plant trail, a fern garden, and rock gardens with unusual plants. The garden is open by reservation only.

11505 SW Summerville Ave. ⒸⒸ **503/636-4112.** www.berrybot.org. Adults $5. Open daylight hours by appointment. Bus: 35 or 36.

Crystal Springs Rhododendron Garden ⚐   Nowhere do rhododendrons do better than in the cool, rainy Northwest, and nowhere in Portland is there a more impressive planting of rhodies than at Crystal Springs. Eight months out of the year, this is a tranquil garden, with a waterfall, a lake, and ducks to feed. But when the rhododendrons and azaleas bloom from March to June, it becomes a spectacular mass of blazing color. The Rhododendron Show and Plant Sale is held here on Mother's Day weekend.

SE 28th Ave. (1 block north of SE Woodstock Blvd.). ⒸⒸ **503/771-8386** or 503/777-1734. Admission $3 Mar 1–Labor Day Thurs–Mon 10am–6pm; free at other times. Open year-round daily dawn–dusk. Bus: 19.

Elk Rock Garden of the Bishop's Close ⚐   Set on a steep hillside above the Willamette River between Portland and Lake Oswego, this was once a private garden but was donated to the local Episcopal bishop of Oregon on the condition that it be opened to the public. The mature gardens are at their best through the spring and early summer. There's also an excellent view of Mount Hood from the grounds.

11800 SW Military Lane. ⒸⒸ **503/636-5613.** Free admission. Daily 8am–5pm. Bus: 35 or 36.

The World's Smallest Park

Don't blink as you cross the median strip on Naito Parkway at the corner of Southwest Taylor Street, or you might just walk right past **Mill Ends Park,** the smallest public park in the world.

Covering a whopping 452.16 square inches of land, this park was the whimsical creation of local journalist Dick Fagen. After a telephone pole was removed from the middle of Naito Parkway (then known as Front Ave.), Fagen dubbed the phone pole hole Mill Ends Park (Mill Ends, a lumber mill term, was the name of Fagen's newspaper column). The columnist, whose office looked down on the hole in the middle of Front Avenue, peopled the imaginary park with leprechauns and would often write of the park's goings-on in his column. On St. Patrick's Day 1976, it was officially designated a Portland city park. Rumor has it that despite its diminutive size, the park has been the site of several weddings (although the parks department has never issued a wedding permit for it).

The Grotto—National Sanctuary of Our Sorrowful Mother
Although this forested 62-acre sanctuary is first and foremost a Catholic religious shrine (with a marble replica of Michelangelo's Pietà set in a shallow rock cave at the foot of a cliff), the gardens are quite beautiful. The gardens are at their best in the early summer and during the Christmas season, when the grounds are decorated with thousands of lights and a choral festival is held. An elevator ride to the top of the bluff offers panoramic views of the Cascade Range, the Columbia River, and Mount St. Helens. There are also a couple of chapels on the grounds, a gift shop, and a coffee shop. The Grotto is open to visitors of all faiths.

NE 85th Ave. and Sandy Blvd. ⓒ **503/254-7371.** www.thegrotto.org. Free admission (except during Christmas Festival of Lights: $6 adults, $3 children 3–12, free for children 2 and under); elevator $2. Open daily summer 9am–7:30pm, winter 9am–4pm, spring 9am–5:30pm. Closed Christmas and Thanksgiving. Bus: 12.

5 Other In-Town Attractions

American Advertising Museum ⚐ Like it or not, advertising is here to stay. In this fun and unusual little museum, you'll learn about its history, from the 1700s to the present, through displays on historic advertisements, celebrities, and jingles. Tapes of old TV commercials provide a popular trip down memory lane. Lots of 20th-century advertising icons are on display, and the most influential ads of the past century are chronicled in detail.

211 NW Fifth Ave. ② **503/226-0000.** www.admuseum.org. Admission $5 adults, $4 seniors and children 4–12. Wed–Sun noon–5pm.

Portland Classical Chinese Garden ★★   This classically styled Chinese garden takes up an entire city block and is the largest of its type outside of China. The walls that surround these gardens in Portland's Chinatown separate the urban 21st century from the timeless Chinese landscape within. This landscape is designed to evoke the wild mountains of China and to create a tranquil oasis within an urban setting. The gardens are centered around a small pond, at one end of which stands a rock wall meant to conjure up the sort of images often seen in Chinese scroll paintings. Numerous pavilions, a small bridge, and a winding pathway provide ever-changing views of the gardens. With its many paved paths and small viewing pavilions, this garden has a completely different feel than the Japanese Garden. Try to visit as soon as the gardens open in the morning; when the crowds descend and the guided tours start circulating—well, so much for tranquillity. Be sure to stop and have a cup of tea and maybe a snack in the garden's tearoom.

NW Everett St. and NW Third Ave. ② **503/228-8131.** Admission $6 adults, $5 seniors, $5 college students and children 6–18, free for children 5 and under. Apr 1–Oct 31 daily 9am–6pm; Nov 1–Mar 31 daily 10am–5pm.

24-Hour Church of Elvis/Where's the Art? *(Finds)*   This is Portland's longtime temple of kitsch, the city's most bizarre attraction. Coin-operated art, a video psychic, cheap (though not legal) weddings, and other absurd assemblages, interactive displays, and kitschy contraptions (such as the Vend-O-Matic Mystery Machine with whirling doll heads) cram this second-floor oddity. As celebrity-spokesmodel/minister S.G. Pierce says, "the tour *is* the art form." If you pass the customer test, you can even buy a Church of Elvis T-shirt. Great fun if you're a fan of Elvis, tabloids, or the unusual; and if you've seen Elvis anytime in the past decade, a visit is absolutely mandatory.

720 SW Ankeny St. ② **503/226-3671.** www.churchofelvis.com. Free admission (with $1 purchase at gift shop). Flexible hours; almost always open on weekends. Any downtown bus.

6 Especially for Kids

In addition to the attractions listed below, the kids will especially enjoy the **Oregon Museum of Science and Industry,** which has lots of hands-on exhibits (p. 86 for details), and the **Oregon Zoo** (p. 90). From inside the zoo, it's possible to take a small train through Washington Park to the International Rose Test Garden, below which there is the **Rose Garden Children's Park,** a colorful play area for younger children. The **Salmon Street Springs fountain,** in downtown's Tom McCall Waterfront Park (at SW Naito Pkwy. and SW Salmon St.), is another fun place to take the kids. During hot summer months, there are always lots of happy kids playing in the jets of water that erupt from the pavement here. There are also big lawns in **Waterfront Park,** so the kids can run off plenty of excess energy.

CM2—Children's Museum 2nd Generation 🎨 *Kids*   Located across the parking lot form the Oregon Zoo, this new children's museum opened in mid-2001. With much more space than the old museum, this "second generation" museum includes exhibits for children from 6 months to 13 years. Kids can experiment with gravity, act out fairy tales, or explore a magical forest. However, it is the Water Works exhibit that is likely to make the biggest splash with your kids. There are also six studios with changing exhibits and opportunities for exploring the visual, literary, and performing arts. Combined with the nearby zoo, this museum now makes for an easy all-day kid-oriented outing.

4015 SW Canyon Rd. ✆ **503/223-6500.** www.portlandcm2.org. Admission $5, free for children under 1 yr. Tues–Thurs 9am–5pm; Fri 9am–8pm; Sun 11am–5pm (open some school holiday Mon). Closed some national holidays. Bus: 63. MAX: Washington Park Station.

Oaks Park Amusement Center *Kids*   What would summer be without the screams of happy thrill-seekers risking life and limb on a roller coaster? Covering more than 44 acres, this amusement park first opened in 1905 to coincide with the Lewis and Clark Exposition. Beneath the shady oaks for which the park is named, you'll find waterfront picnic sites, miniature golf, music, and plenty of thrilling rides. Check out the largest wood-floored roller-skating rink in the west where an organist still plays the Wurlitzer for the skaters.

East end of the Sellwood Bridge. ✆ **503/233-5777.** www.oakspark.com. Free admission; individual-ride tickets $1.50, limited-ride bracelet $9.75, deluxe-ride bracelet $12.25. Mid-June to Labor Day Tues–Thurs noon–9pm, Fri–Sat noon–10pm, Sun noon–7pm (separate hours for skating rink); May to mid-June and Sept (after Labor Day) Sat–Sun noon–7pm (weather allowing). Bus: 40.

7 Organized Tours

CRUISES

If you'd like to see the city from either the Columbia or the Willamette rivers, you've got plenty of options. Traditionalists will want to book a tour on the **Sternwheeler *Columbia Gorge*** (© 503/223-3928), which offers sternwheeler cruises through Portland on the Willamette River between October and late June. During the summer months, this boat operates out of Cascade Locks on the Columbia River and does trips in the scenic Columbia Gorge. Although it's fun to see the city from the water, the summer trips beneath the towering cliffs of the Columbia Gorge are far more impressive—a definite must on a summertime visit to Portland. Two-hour cruises are $14.95 for adults and $8.95 for children. Call for information on brunch, dinner, and dance cruises.

If a modern yacht is more your speed, try the ***Portland Spirit*** (© 800/224-3901 or 503/224-3900; www.portlandspirit.com). This 75-foot yacht specializes in dinner cruises and seats 350 people on two decks. Lunch, brunch, and dinner cruises feature Northwest cuisine with views of the city skyline. Saturday nights the *Portland Spirit* becomes a floating nightclub with live bands or a DJ, and there are also Friday afternoon cocktail cruises in the summer. Call for reservations and schedule. Prices range from $15 to $52 for adults and $9 to $47 for children.

For high-speed tours up the Willamette River, there are the **Willamette Jetboat Excursions** (© 888/JETBOAT or 503/231-1532; www.jetboatpdx.com). The high-powered open-air boats blast their way from downtown Portland to the impressive Willamette Falls at Oregon City. The 2-hour tours, which start at OMSI, are $25 for adults and $15 for children 4 to 11, free for 3 and under. Tours are offered from May to mid-October.

BUS TOURS

If you want to get a general overview of Portland, **Gray Line** (© 800/422-7042 or 503/285-9845) offers several half-day and full-day tours. One itinerary takes in the International Rose Test Garden and the grounds of Pittock Mansion; another stops at the Japanese Garden and the World Forestry Center. There are also tours up to see the waterfalls in the Columbia Gorge, to Mount

Hood, and to the Oregon coast. Tour prices range from $27 to $47 for adults, and from $13.50 to $23.50 for children.

RAIL EXCURSIONS

While Portland is busy reviving trolleys as a viable mass transit option, the **Willamette Shore Trolley** ⚘ (📞 503/222-2226) is offering scenic excursions along the Willamette River in historic trolley cars (including a double-decker) from the early part of this century. The old wooden trolleys rumble over trestles and through a tunnel as they cover the 7 miles between Portland and the prestigious suburb of Lake Oswego (a 45-min. trip). Along the way, you pass through shady corridors with lots of views of the river and glimpses into the yards of posh riverfront homes. In Lake Oswego, the trolley station is on State Street, between "A" Avenue and Foothills Road. In downtown Portland, the station is just south of the RiverPlace Athletic Club on Harbor Way (off Naito Pkwy. at the south end of Tom McCall Waterfront Park). The round-trip fare is $8 for adults, $7 for seniors, and $4 for children 3 to 12. Call for a schedule. They also do an annual Fourth of July fireworks run from Oaks Park on the east bank of the Willamette River, and a Christmas run to see the Holiday Parade of Ships.

WALKING TOURS

Peter's Walking Tours of Portland (📞 **503/665-2558** or 503/680-4296; famchausse@aol.com), led by university instructor Peter Chausse, are a great way to learn more about Portland. The walking tours of downtown take 2½ hours, cover about 1½ miles, and take in the city's fountains, parks, historic places, art, and architecture. Tours are by reservation and cost $10 for adults (children 12 and under free with a paying adult).

Two to three times a year, Sharon Wood Wortman, author of *The Portland Bridge Book,* offers a **Bridge Tour and Urban Adventure** that explores several Portland bridges. These tours are offered through the Outdoor Recreation Program of **Portland Parks and Recreation** (📞 **503/823-5132**). Many other walking tours are also available through Portland Parks and Recreation.

The seamy underbelly of history is laid bare on **Portland Underground Tours** ⚘ (📞 **503/622-4798**), which head down below street level in the historic Old Town neighborhood. On these unusual tours, which are only for those who are steady on their feet and able to duck under pipes and joists and such, you'll hear tales of the days when Portland was known as one of the most dangerous ports on the Pacific Rim. Sailors were regularly shanghaied from bars and brothels in this area and a vast network of tunnels and underground rooms developed to support the shanghaiing business. Tours cost $10 and are offered on an irregular basis. Reservations are required.

WINERY TOURS

If you're interested in learning more about Oregon wines and want to tour the nearby wine country with a guide, contact **Grape Escape** (© 503/283-3380; www.grapeescapetours.com), which offers an in-depth winery tour of the Willamette Valley. All-day tours include stops at several wineries, appetizers, lunch, and dessert, and pickup and drop-off at your hotel ($85 per person). For people with less time, there are half-day afternoon trips that take in two or three wineries ($60 per person). A number of other tours are also available.

For information on touring wine country on your own, see "A Winery Tour" in chapter 10, "Side Trips from Portland."

8 Outdoor Pursuits

If you're planning ahead for a visit to Portland, contact **Metro Regional Parks and Greenspaces,** 600 NE Grand Ave., Portland, OR 97232-2736 (© **503/797-1850;** www.metro-region.org), for its *Metro GreenScene* publication that lists tours, hikes, classes, and other outdoor activities and events being held in the Portland metro area.

BEACHES

The nearest ocean beaches are **Cannon Beach** (a charming village) and **Seaside** (an old-fashioned family beach town), about 90 miles to the west. See "The Northern Oregon Coast" in chapter 10, "Side Trips from Portland," for more information.

There are a couple of freshwater beaches on the Columbia River within 45 minutes of Portland. **Rooster Rock State Park,** just off I-84 east of Portland, includes several miles of sandy beach as does **Sauvie Island,** off Oregon Hwy. 30 northwest of Portland. You'll need to obtain a parking permit for Sauvie Island; it's available at the convenience store located just after you cross the bridge onto the island. Both beaches include clothing-optional sections, though these are well separated from the more popular clothing-required beaches.

BIKING

Portland is a very bicycle-friendly city, and you'll notice plenty of bikers on the streets. There are also lots of miles of paved bike paths around the city, and some good mountain biking areas as well. There aren't too many choices for rentals, but try **Fat Tire Farm,** 2714 NW Thurman St. (© **503/222-3276**), where you can get a mountain bike for $40 a day. Straight up Thurman Street from the bike shop, you'll find the trail head for the **Leif Ericson Trail,** and old gravel road that is Forest Park's favorite route for cyclists and runners (the road is closed to motor vehicles); the trail is 12 miles long.

GOLF

If you're a golfer, don't forget to bring your clubs along on a trip to Portland. There are plenty of public courses around the area, and greens fees at municipal courses are as low as $21 for 18 holes on a weekday and $35 on weekends and holidays. Municipal golf courses operated by the Portland Bureau of Parks and Recreation include **Redtail Golf Course,** 8200 SW Scholls Ferry Rd. (© **503/646-5166**); **Eastmoreland Golf Course,** 2425 SE Bybee Blvd. (© **503/775-2900**), which is the second oldest golf course in the state (this one gets our vote for best municipal course); **Heron Lakes Golf Course,** 3500 N. Victory Blvd. (© **503/289-1818**), a Robert Trent Jones design; and **Rose City Golf Course,** 2200 NE 71st Ave. (© **503/253-4744**), on the site of a former country club. If you want to tee off where the pros play, head west from Portland 20 miles to **Pumpkin Ridge Golf Club** 🐦🐦, 12930 NW Old Pumpkin Ridge Rd. (© **503/647-4747**), which has hosted the U.S. Women's Open. Greens fees are $120 ($135 with cart) and $65 after 3pm Monday through Thursday.

Also west of the city, on the south side of Hillsboro, you'll find the **Reserve Vineyards & Golf Club** 🐦🐦, 4805 SW 229th Ave.,

Impressions

*While the people of Portland are not mercurial or excitable—
and by Californians or people "east of the mountains"
are even accused of being lymphatic, if not somnolent—
they are much given . . . to recreation and public
amusements.*

—Harvey Scott, editor of the *Oregonian,* 1890

Aloha (© **503/649-8191;** www.reservegolf.com). Greens fees are $65 Monday through Thursday and $79 Friday through Sunday.

HIKING

Hiking opportunities in the Portland area are almost unlimited. For shorter hikes, you need not leave the city. Bordered by West Burnside Street on the south, Newberry Road on the north, St. Helens Road on the east, and Skyline Road on the west, **Forest Park** is the largest forested city park in the country. You'll find more than 50 miles of trails through this urban wilderness. One of our favorite access points is at the top of NW Thurman Street in northwest Portland. (After a hike, you can stop by one of the neighborhood brewpubs, an espresso bar, or bakery along NW 23rd or NW 21st Ave. for a post-exercise payoff.) The Wildwood Trail is the longest trail in the park and offers the most options for loop hikes along its length. For a roughly 2½-mile hike, head up Leif Ericson Drive to a left onto the Wild Cherry Trail to a right onto the Wildwood Trail to a right onto the Dogwood Trail, and then a right on Leif Ericson Drive to get you back to the trail head. There are also good sections of trail to hike in the vicinity of the Hoyt Arboretum. To reach the arboretum's visitor center, 4000 SW Fairview Boulevard (open daily 9am–3pm), drive west on West Burnside Street from downtown Portland and follow signs to the arboretum. You can get a trail map here at the visitor center.

About 5 miles south of downtown, you'll find **Tryon Creek State Park** on Terwilliger Road. This park is similar to Forest Park and is best known for its displays of trillium flowers in the spring. There are several miles of walking trails within the park, and a bike path to downtown Portland starts here.

You can buy or rent camping equipment from **REI Co-Op,** 1798 Jantzen Beach Center (© **503/283-1300**), or 7410 SW Bridgeport Rd., Tualatin (© **503/624-8600**). This huge outdoor recreation supply store also sells books on hiking in the area.

SEA KAYAKING

If you want to check out the Portland skyline from water level, arrange for a sea kayak tour through the **Portland River Company** ⚔⚔, 0315 SW Montgomery St. (© **888/238-2059** or 503/229-0551; www.portlandrivercompany.com), which operates out of the RiverPlace Marina at the south end of Tom McCall Waterfront Park. A 2½-hour tour that circles nearby Ross Island costs $35 per person. All-day trips on the lower Columbia River are also offered ($75 per person) and will get you off an urban river and into a wildlife refuge. This company also rents sea kayaks (to experienced paddlers) for $15 to $20 for the first hour and $10 to $15 per hour after that.

SKIING

There are several ski resorts within about an hour's drive of Portland, on the slopes of Mount Hood. Timberline Ski Area even boasts summer skiing. There are also many miles of marked cross-country ski trails. The best cross-country skiing on Mount Hood is at the Nordic center at Mount Hood Meadows, and at Teacup Lake, which is along Ore. 35 near the turnoff for Mount Hood Meadows. You'll find numerous ski and snowboard rental shops in the town of Sandy, which is on the way from Portland to Mount Hood, and ski areas also rent equipment.

Timberline Ski Area *(℗ **503/272-3311** for information, or 503/222-2211 for snow report; www.timberlinelodge.com) is the highest ski area on Mount Hood and has one slope that is open all the way through summer. This is the site of the historic Timberline Lodge, which was built during the Depression by the WPA. Adult lift ticket prices range from $18 for night skiing to $37 for an all-day pass. Call for hours of operation.

Mount Hood Meadows *(℗ **503/337-2222,** or 503/ 227-7669 for snow report; www.skihood.com) is the largest ski resort on Mount Hood, with more than 2,000 skiable acres, 2,777 vertical feet, and a wide variety of terrain. Lift ticket prices range from $18 for night skiing to $41 for a weekend all-day pass. Call for hours of operation.

Mt. Hood SkiBowl *(℗ **503/272-3206,** or 503/222-2695 for snow report; www.skibowl.com), the closest ski area to Portland, offers 1,500 vertical feet of skiing and has more expert slopes than any other ski area on the mountain. SkiBowl is also one of the largest lighted ski areas in the country. Adult lift ticket prices range from $18 for midweek night skiing to $31 for a weekend all-day pass. Call for hours of operation.

All of the ski areas mentioned above allow snowboarding. Mount Hood Meadows and Mt. Hood SkiBowl both have cross-country skiing (though only Mount Hood Meadows has a Nordic Center and groomed fee-access trails).

TENNIS

Portland Parks and Recreation operates more than 120 tennis courts, both indoors and out, all over the city. Outdoor courts are generally free and available on a first-come, first-served basis. Our personal favorites are those in Washington Park just behind the International Rose Test Garden. If you want to be certain of getting a particular court time, some of these courts can be reserved by contacting Portland Parks and Recreation at ℂ **503/823-2525,** ext. 6.

If the weather isn't cooperating, head for the **Portland Tennis Center,** 324 NE 12th Ave. (ℂ **503/823-3189**). They have indoor courts and charge about $5.75 to $7.75 per hour per person for singles matches and $3.75 to $5 per hour per person for doubles.

WHITE-WATER RAFTING

The Cascade Range produces some of the best white-water rafting in the country, and the Deschutes, White Salmon, Sandy, and Clackamas rivers all offer plenty of opportunities to shoot within an hour or two of Portland. The Sandy and the Clackamas are the two closest rivers.

Portland River Company, 0315 SW Montgomery St. (ℂ **888/ 238-2059** or 503/229-0551; www.portlandrivercompany.com), offers day trips on the Deschutes and North Umpqua rivers ($75 per person) and 2- to 3-day trips on the Deschutes River ($260–$360 per person). Trips on the Sandy, Clackamas, North Santiam, and Hood rivers are offered by **Blue Sky Whitewater Rafting** (ℂ **800/898-6398;** www.blueskyrafting.com), which charges $30 to $35 for a half-day trip and $55 to $60 for a full-day trip. **River Drifters** (ℂ **800/972-0430** or 800/226-1001; www. riverdrifters.net) offers trips on the Deschutes, White Salmon, Clackamas, Wind River, North Santiam, and Klickitat rivers for between $65 and $75 for a full day. **Zoller's Outdoor Odysseys, Inc.,** 1248 Hwy. 141, White Salmon, WA (ℂ **800/366-2004** or 509/493-2641; www.zooraft.com), offers trips on the White Salmon for $60.

If you already have some rafting experience and just want to rent a raft for the easy Class 1-plus rapids on the lower Sandy River (between Oxbow Park and Dabney Park), contact **River Trails,** 336 E Columbia River Hwy., Troutdale (ℂ **503/667-1964**), which charges $50 per day for a four-person raft.

9 Spectator Sports

Tickets to most games, including those of the Trail Blazers, the Portland Winter Hawks, and the Portland Beavers, are sold through **Ticketmaster** (ℂ **503/224-4400;** www.ticketmaster.com).

Tickets to events at the Rose Garden arena and Memorial Coliseum are also sold through the **Rose Quarter** box office (© **503/797-9617** for tickets; 503/321-3211 event information hot line; www.rosequarter.com). The Rose Garden arena is home to the Portland Trail Blazers and the Portland Winter Hawks and is the main focal point of Portland's **Rose Quarter.** This sports and entertainment neighborhood is still more an idea than a reality, but it does include the Rose Garden, Memorial Coliseum, and several restaurants and bars. To reach the Rose Garden or adjacent Memorial Coliseum, take the Rose Quarter exit off I-5. Parking is expensive, so you might want to consider taking the MAX light-rail line from downtown Portland.

AUTO RACING   **Portland International Raceway,** West Delta Park, 1940 N. Victory Blvd. (© **503/823-RACE**), hosts road races, drag races, motocross and other motorcycle races, go-kart races, and even vintage-car races. February through October are the busiest months here.

BASEBALL   The **Portland Beavers Baseball Club** (© **503/553-5555;** www.pgepark.com), the AAA affiliate of the San Diego Padres, plays minor-league ball at the recently renovated PGE Park, SW 20th Avenue and Morrison Street. Tickets are $3.25 to $8.75.

BASKETBALL   The NBA's **Portland Trail Blazers** (© **503/231-8000** or 503/234-9291; www.nba.com/blazers) do well enough each year to have earned them a very loyal following. Unfortunately, they have a habit of not quite making it all the way to the top. The mercurial Rasheed Wallace and his fellow Blazers pound the boards at the Rose Garden arena. Call for current schedule and ticket information. Tickets are $10 to $127. If the Blazers are doing well, you can bet that tickets will be hard to come by.

10 Day Spas

If you'd rather opt for a massage than a hike in the woods, consider spending a few hours at a day spa. These facilities typically offer massages, facials, seaweed wraps, and the like. Portland day spas include **Aveda Lifestyle Store and Spa,** 5th Avenue Suites Hotel, 500 Washington St. (© **503/248-0615**); **Urbaca,** 120 NW Ninth Ave., Suite 101 (© **503/241-5030**); and **Salon Nyla—The Day Spa,** adjacent to the Embassy Suites hotel at 327 SW Pine St. (© **503/228-0389**). Expect to pay about $65 to $75 for a 1-hour massage and $150 to $435 for a multitreatment spa package.

7

Strolling Around Portland

Portland's compactness makes it an ideal city to explore on foot. There's no better way to gain a feel for this city than to stroll through the Skidmore Historic District, down along Tom McCall Waterfront Park, and through Pioneer Courthouse Square. If you're here on the weekend, you'll also be able to visit the Portland Saturday Market. For additional information on several stops in this stroll, see chapter 6, "Exploring Portland."

WALKING TOUR	OLD TOWN & DOWNTOWN

Start:	Skidmore Fountain
Finish:	Skidmore Fountain
Time:	Allow approximately 3 to 4 hours, including breaks, museum visits, and shopping stops
Best Times:	Saturday and Sunday between March and December, when the Portland Saturday Market is open
Worst Times:	After dark, when the Skidmore neighborhood is not as safe as in daylight

Although Portland was founded in 1843, most of the buildings in Old Town date only from the 1880s. A fire in 1872 razed much of the town, which afterward was rebuilt with new vigor. Ornate pilasters, pediments, and cornices grace these brick buildings. However, the most notable features of Old Town's buildings are the cast-iron facades.

Begin your exploration of this 20-block historic neighborhood in the heart of Old Town. At the corner of SW First Avenue and Ankeny Street is:

❶ Skidmore Fountain

Erected in 1888, the fountain was intended to provide refreshment for "horses, men, and dogs," and it did that for many years. Today, however, the bronze and granite fountain is primarily decorative.

Walking Tour: Old Town & Downtown

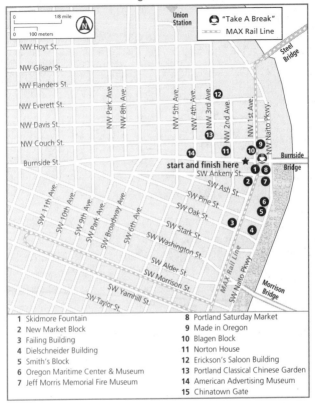

1 Skidmore Fountain
2 New Market Block
3 Failing Building
4 Dielschneider Building
5 Smith's Block
6 Oregon Maritime Center & Museum
7 Jeff Morris Memorial Fire Museum
8 Portland Saturday Market
9 Made in Oregon
10 Blagen Block
11 Norton House
12 Erickson's Saloon Building
13 Portland Classical Chinese Garden
14 American Advertising Museum
15 Chinatown Gate

Across SW First Avenue is the:

② New Market Block

Constructed in 1872 to house the unlikely combination of a produce market and a theater, the New Market Block contains some unusual shops and budget restaurants, as do many of the restored historic buildings in this area. The free-standing wall of archways extending out from the New Market Building was salvaged from an Old Town structure that didn't survive the urban renewal craze of the 1960s.

Two blocks south, at 235 SW First Ave., is the:

❸ Failing Building

Built in 1886, this attractive structure integrates French and Italian influences. (This building houses McCormick and Schmick's seafood restaurant, a good place for lunch if the Sat Market is closed.)

Turn left on SW Oak Street and you'll pass by the:

❹ Dielschneider Building

This structure at 71 SW Oak St. was originally a foundry. Built in 1859, it's the third oldest commercial building in Portland. The casting initials of one of the first tenants, Oregon Ironworks, can be seen on the building's threshold plates.

Take a left on SW Naito Parkway (Front Ave.) where you'll find:

❺ Smith's Block

Located from 111–117 SW Naito Parkway, it contains some of the most beautifully restored buildings in Old Town. At one time this whole district was filled with elegant structures such as these. The cast-iron filigree appears both solid and airy at the same time.

Here, at 113 SW Naito Pkwy., you'll find the:

❻ Oregon Maritime Center and Museum

This museum is dedicated to Oregon's shipping history. See the complete listing in chapter 6 for details.

Continue along SW Naito Parkway to SW Ankeny, where you'll see the:

❼ Jeff Morris Memorial Fire Museum

It houses several pieces of old fire-fighting equipment, including historic horse-drawn steamers from the early part of the 20th century. Because this museum is part of an active fire station and because the equipment is packed so tightly together, you can't actually go inside the museum. You'll have to be satisfied with looking through the glass doors that face the street.

If it's a Saturday or Sunday between March and December, you will no doubt have noticed the crowds under the Burnside Bridge ahead of you. This is the:

❽ Portland Saturday Market

Here you'll find the best of Northwest crafts being sold by their makers. There typically are more than 250 booths plus entertainers and food vendors. See the complete listing in chapter 6, "Exploring Portland," for more details.

TAKE A BREAK
Portland Saturday Market makes an excellent refueling stop in this neighborhood. In the market's food court you can get all manner of delicious, healthful, and fun foods.

After you've visited the market, walk north on the east side of NW First Avenue. Just out from under the shadow of the Burnside Bridge, at 10 NW First Ave., you'll find:

9 Made in Oregon

This shop sells all things Oregon, from Pendleton blankets to local wines. This is a great place to pick up more gifts if you haven't already spent more than you should have at the Saturday Market.

From here, continue up NW First Avenue to the corner of NW Couch (pronounced *Kooch*) Street, where you'll find the:

10 Blagen Block

This is another excellent example of the ornate cast-iron facades that appeared on nearly all the buildings in this area at one time. Note the cast-iron figures of women wearing spiked crowns. They are reminiscent of the Statue of Liberty, which was erected 2 years before this building opened in 1888.

Across First Avenue, you'll see the covered sidewalk of the:

11 Norton House

Though this is not the original covered sidewalk, it is characteristic of Portland buildings from 100 years ago.

Walk west to Second Avenue, where at the southwest corner you'll see:

12 Erickson's Saloon Building

Back in the late 1800s this building at 9 NW Second Ave. housed the very popular Erickson's Saloon, with a 684-foot-long bar, card rooms, and a brothel.

From here, walk north on Second Avenue to the corner of Everett Street and turn left. At the corner of Everett Street and Third Avenue, you'll find the:

13 Portland Classical Chinese Garden

This is the largest classical Suzhou-style Chinese garden outside of China. With its tiled roofs, pond, bridges, and landscaping that conjures up images from Chinese scroll paintings, the garden is an urban oasis. See the listing in chapter 6 for more information.

From here, walk back south on NW Third Avenue to the corner of Davis Street, turn right, and in 2 blocks, you'll see, on the northwest corner, the:

⓮ American Advertising Museum

Located at 211 NW Fifth Ave., this museum houses fun displays on the history of advertising. Inside, you can watch videos of some of the most unforgettable TV commercials of the past 50 years, follow the history of advertising in the United States, and get face to face with the likes of Aunt Jemima, Mr. Peanut, and Big Boy. See the complete listing in chapter 6, "Exploring Portland."

From here, walk back to Fourth Avenue, turn right, and ahead of you, at the corner of Fourth Avenue and Burnside Street, you'll see the:

⓯ Chinatown Gate

Since you're already in Chinatown, you'll have to cross to the opposite side of the brightly painted three-tiered gateway to appreciate its ornate design, including two huge flanking bronze Chinese lions.

From here, cross West Burnside Street, turn left on Ankeny, and walk 3 blocks back to the Skidmore Fountain to end the tour.

8

Portland Shopping

Portland has no sales tax, making it a popular shopping destination for Washingtonians, who cross the Columbia River to avoid paying their state's substantial sales tax.

1 The Shopping Scene

The **blocks around Pioneer Courthouse Square** are the heartland of upscale shopping in Portland. It's here that you'll find Nordstrom, NIKETOWN, Saks Fifth Avenue, Tiffany, Pioneer Place shopping mall, and numerous upscale boutiques and shops.

However, Portland's hippest shopping district is the **Nob Hill/ Northwest neighborhood along NW 23rd Avenue beginning at West Burnside Street.** Here you'll find block after block of unusual boutiques as well as such chains as Gap, Urban Outfitters, and Pottery Barn.

For shops with a more down-to-earth, funky flavor, head out to the **Hawthorne District,** which is the city's counterculture shopping area (lots of tie-dye and imports).

In the **Pearl District,** of which NW Glisan Street and NW 10th Avenue are the center, you'll find the city's greatest concentration of art galleries.

Most small stores in Portland are open Monday through Saturday from 9 or 10am to 5 or 6pm. Shopping malls are usually open Monday through Friday from 9 or 10am to 9pm, Saturday from 9 or 10am to between 6 and 9pm, and Sunday from 11am until 6pm. Many department stores stay open past 6pm. Most art galleries and antiques stores are closed on Monday.

2 Shopping A to Z
ANTIQUES

The **Sellwood** neighborhood (south of downtown at the east end of the Sellwood Bridge) is Portland's main antiques-shopping district, with about 30 antiques shops and antiques malls along 12 blocks of

SE 13th Avenue. With its old Victorian homes and 19th-century architecture, Sellwood is an ideal setting for these shops. There are plenty of good restaurants in the area in case it turns into an all-day outing.

You'll also find three more large antiques malls (all under the same ownership) nearby on Milwaukie Boulevard: **Stars,** at 6717 SE Milwaukie Blvd. (✆ **503/235-9142**), and at 7027 SE Milwaukie Blvd. (✆ **503/239-0346**); and **Star & Splendid,** 7030 SE Milwaukie Blvd. (✆ **503/235-5990**).

ART GALLERIES

On the **first Thursday of the month,** galleries in downtown Portland schedule coordinated openings in the evening. Stroll from one gallery to the next, meeting artists and perhaps buying an original work of art.

A guide listing dozens of Portland galleries is available at galleries around the city.

GENERAL ART GALLERIES

Augen Gallery   When it opened 17 years ago, the Augen Gallery focused on internationally recognized artists such as Jim Dine, Andy Warhol, and David Hockney. Today, the gallery has expanded its repertoire to regional contemporary painters and printmakers as well. 817 SW Second Ave. ✆ **503/224-8182.** www.augengallery.com.

Blackfish Gallery   Artist-owned since 1979, the Blackfish is a large and relaxing space featuring contemporary images. Since this gallery is a cooperative, it doesn't have the same constraints as a commercial art gallery and thus can present more cutting-edge and thought-provoking work. 420 NW Ninth Ave. ✆ **503/224-2634.**

The Laura Russo Gallery   The focus here is on Northwest contemporary artists, showcasing talented emerging artists as well as the estates of well-known artists. Laura Russo has been on the Portland art scene for a long time and is highly respected. 805 NW 21st Ave. ✆ **503/226-2754.**

Margo Jacobsen Gallery   In the heart of the Pearl District, this gallery is where you'll find most of the crowds milling about on First Thursdays. Margo Jacobsen promotes contemporary painters, printmakers, and photographers, with a focus on ceramics and glass. 1039 NW Glisan St. ✆ **503/224-7287.**

Pulliam Deffenbaugh Gallery   This gallery represents a long list of both talented newcomers and masters from the Northwest.

The City of Books

Portland's own **Powell's City of Books,** 1005 W. Burnside St. (© 503/228-4651 or 800/878-7323; www.powells.com), is the bookstore to end all bookstores. Powell's, which covers an entire city block three floors deep, claims to be the world's largest bookstore. Those books, roughly three-quarters of a million at any given time, are shelved side by side—well-thumbed old paperbacks next to the latest hardcover books—which is why browsing is what Powell's is all about.

Once inside the store, be sure to pick up a store map, which will direct you to the color-coded rooms. In the Gold Room, you'll find science fiction and mysteries. The Rose Room has books on ornithology, the outdoors, and sports, among other subjects, as well as children's books. In the Orange Room, there are books on cooking, gardening, business, and crafts. Serious book collectors won't want to miss a visit to the Rare Book Room.

One warning: If you haven't got at least an hour of free time, enter at your own risk. It's so easy to lose track of time at Powell's that many customers miss meals and end up in the store's in-house cafe.

Believe it or not, City of Books is even bigger than what you see here; it has several satellite stores. There's **Powell's Technical Bookstore,** 33 NW Park St. (© 503/228-3906); **Powell's Books for Cooks and Gardeners,** 3747 SE Hawthorne Blvd. (© 503/235-3802); **Powell's Books on Hawthorne,** 3723 SE Hawthorne Blvd. (© 503/238-1668); **Powell's Travel Store,** Pioneer Courthouse Square, SW Sixth Avenue and Yamhill Street (© 503/228-1108); **Powell's Books in Beaverton,** at the Progress exit off Ore. 217 in Beaverton (© 503/643-3131); and **Powell's Books at PDX,** Portland International Airport (© 503/249-1950).

Solo shows and salon-style group shows are held here at the Pearl District location, and also at the Pulliam Deffenbaugh Broadway Gallery downtown at 507 SW Broadway (© 503/228-8208). 522 NW 12th Ave. © 503/228-6665.

Quintana Galleries   This large, bright space is virtually a small museum of Native-American art, selling everything from Northwest Indian masks to contemporary paintings and sculptures by various Northwest coast Indian and Inuit artists. They also carry a smattering of Northwest and Southwest Indian antiquities. The jewelry selection is outstanding. Prices, however, are not cheap. 501 SW Broadway. ☎ 503/223-1729.

ART GLASS

The Bullseye Connection   Located in the Pearl District, the Bullseye Connection is a large open exhibition and sales space for glass artists. Pieces sold here include sculptures, delightful glass jewelry, paperweights, and even marbles. There's even a Dale Chihuly chandelier of pink fruit-like objects on display. Workshops and lectures related to glassmaking are also offered. The **Bullseye Connection Gallery,** which is across the street at 300 NW 13th St. (☎ **503/227-0222**), shows work of internationally acclaimed glass artists. 1308 NW Everett St. ☎ **503/227-2797.**

BOOKS

Major chain bookstores in Portland include **Barnes & Noble** at 1231 NE Broadway (☎ **503/335-0201**) and 1720 Jantzen Beach Center (☎ **503/283-2800**), and **Borders** at 708 SW Third Ave. (☎ **503/220-5911**).

CRAFTS

For the largest selection of local crafts, visit the **Portland Saturday Market** (see "Markets," below), which is a showcase for local crafts.

Contemporary Crafts Gallery   In business since 1937 and located in a residential area between downtown and the John's Landing neighborhood, this is the nation's oldest nonprofit art gallery showing exclusively artwork in clay, glass, fiber, metal, and wood. The bulk of the large gallery is taken up by glass and ceramic pieces in ongoing thematic exhibitions. There are also several cabinets of jewelry. 3934 SW Corbett Ave. ☎ **503/223-2654.**

Graystone Gallery   This gallery in the Hawthorne district is full of fun and whimsical artwork and home furnishings, including paintings, jewelry, ceramics, and greeting cards. 3279 SE Hawthorne Blvd. ☎ **503/238-0651.**

Hoffman Gallery   The Hoffman Gallery is on the campus of the Oregon College of Art and Craft, one of the nation's foremost crafts education centers since 1906. The gallery hosts installations and group shows by local, national, and international artists. The adjacent gift shop has a good selection of handcrafted items. The grounds are serene and relaxing, and there is also a cafe. 8245 SW Barnes Rd. ✆ **503/297-5544.**

The Real Mother Goose This is Portland's premier fine crafts shop and one of the top such shops in the United States. It showcases only the very best contemporary American crafts, including imaginative ceramics, colorful art glass, intricate jewelry, exquisite wooden furniture, and sculptural works. Hundreds of craftspeople and artists from all over the United States are represented here. There are also locations at Washington Square; Tigard (✆ **503/620-2243**); and Portland International Airport, Main Terminal (✆ **503/284-9929**). 901 SW Yamhill St. ✆ **503/223-9510.** www.thereal mothergoose.com. Also at Washington Square; Tigard (✆ **503/620-2243**); and Portland International Airport, Main Terminal (✆ **503/284-9929**).

Twist This large store has quite a massive selection of wildly colorful and imaginative furniture, crockery, glassware, and lamps, and also a limited but intense selection of handmade jewelry from artists around the United States. Pioneer Place, 700 SW Fifth Ave. ✆ **503/222-3137.** Also at 30 NW 23rd Place (✆ **503/224-0334**).

DEPARTMENT STORES

Meier and Frank Meier and Frank is a Portland institution and has been doing business here for more than 100 years. The flagship store on Pioneer Courthouse Square was built in 1898 and, with 10 stories, was at one time the tallest store in the Northwest. Today those 10 floors of consumer goods and great sales still attract crowds of shoppers. The store is open daily, with Friday usually the latest night. 621 SW Fifth Ave. ✆ **503/223-0512.** Also at 1100 Lloyd Center (✆ **503/281-4797**) and 9300 SW Washington Square Rd. in Tigard (✆ **503/620-3311**).

Nordstrom Directly across the street from Pioneer Courthouse Square and a block away from Meier and Frank, Nordstrom is a top-of-the-line department store that originated in the Northwest and takes great pride in its personal service and friendliness. 701 SW Broadway. ✆ **503/224-6666.** Also at 1001 Lloyd Center (✆ **503/287-2444**) and 9700 SW Washington Square Rd. in Tigard (✆ **503/620-0555**).

FASHION
SPORTSWEAR

Columbia Sportswear Company This flagship store is surprisingly low-key, given that the nearby Nike flagship store and the new

REI in Seattle are designed to knock your socks off. Displays showing the Columbia line of outdoor clothing are rustic, with lots of natural wood. The most dramatic architectural feature of the store is the entryway, in which a very wide tree trunk seems to support the roof. 911 SW Broadway. ✆ **503/226-6800.**

Columbia Sportswear Company Outlet Store *Value*   This outlet store in the Sellwood neighborhood south of downtown and across the river sells well-made outdoor clothing and sportswear from one of the Northwest's premiere outdoor clothing manufacturers. You'll pay 30% to 50% less here than you will at the downtown flagship store (though the clothes will likely be last year's). 1323 SE Tacoma St. ✆ **503/238-0118.**

The Jantzen Store   Jantzen is another of Portland's famous sportswear manufacturers. The full line of attractive and innovative swimsuit styles are sold right here, and there are even occasional sales. 921 SW Morrison St. (in the Galleria). ✆ **503/221-1443.** www.jantzen.com.

Nike Portland Factory Store *Value*   The Nike outlet is one season behind the current season at NIKETOWN (see below), selling swoosh brand running, aerobic, tennis, golf, basketball, kids, and you-name-it sports clothing and accessories at discounted prices. 2650 NE Martin Luther King Jr. Blvd. ✆ **503/281-5901.**

NIKETOWN   Sure, you may have a NIKETOWN back home, but this one is the closest to Nike's headquarters in nearby Beaverton, which somehow makes it just a little bit special. Matte black decor, kinetic displays, and edgy music give NIKETOWN the feel of a sports museum or disco. A true shopping experience. 930 SW Sixth Ave. ✆ **503/221-6453.**

MEN'S & WOMEN'S

Langlitz Leathers   This family-run shop produces the Rolls Royce of leather jackets. Even though there may be a wait (the shop turns out only six handmade jackets a day), motorcyclists ride their Harleys all the way from the East Coast to be fitted. It's rumored that Jay Leno once bought a jacket here. 2443 SE Division St. ✆ **503/ 235-0959.**

Norm Thompson   Known throughout the country for its mail-order catalogs, Norm Thompson is a mainstay of the well-to-do in Portland. Classic styling for men and women is the name of the game here. 1805 NW Thurman St. ✆ **503/221-0764.** Also at Portland International Airport (✆ **503/249-0170**).

The Portland Pendleton Shop   Pendleton wool is as much a part of life in the Northwest as forests and salmon. This company's fine wool fashions for men and women define the country-club look in the Northwest and in many other parts of the country. Pleated skirts and tweed jackets are de rigueur here, as are the colorful blankets that have warmed generations of Northwesterners through long chilly winters. 900 SW Fifth Ave. (entrance is actually on Fourth Ave. between Salmon and Taylor). ✆ **503/242-0037.**

WOMEN'S CLOTHING

Byrkit   Byrkit specializes in natural fabric clothing of cotton, silk, rayon, and linen for women. The contemporary designs, including dresses, jumpers, and separates, are comfortable but still stylish. 2200 NE Broadway. ✆ **503/282-3773.**

Changes   This shop specializes in handmade clothing, including hand-woven scarves, jackets, shawls, hand-painted silks, and other wearable art. 927 SW Yamhill St. ✆ **503/223-3737.**

The Eye of Ra   Women with sophisticated tastes in ethnic fashions will want to visit this shop in The Water Tower at John's Landing shopping center. Silk and rayon predominate, and there's ethnic jewelry by creative designers. Ethnic furniture and home decor are also sold. 5331 SW Macadam Ave. ✆ **503/224-4292.**

M. Sellin Ltd.   Located in the relaxed and low-key Hawthorne district, this shop carries women's "soft dressing" clothing made of natural fabrics with comfortable styling by designers such as Mishi and Amanda Gray. There's also a good selection of jewelry at reasonable prices. 3556 SE Hawthorne Blvd. ✆ **503/239-4605.**

FOOD

The **Made in Oregon** shops offer the best selection of local food products. See "Gifts & Souvenirs," below, for details.

GIFTS & SOUVENIRS

For unique locally made souvenirs, your best bet is the **Portland Saturday Market** (see "Markets," below, for details).

Made in Oregon   This is your one-stop shop for all manner of made-in-Oregon gifts, food products, and clothing. Every product sold is either grown, caught, or made in Oregon. You'll find smoked salmon, filberts, jams and jellies, Pendleton woolens, and Oregon wines. All branches are open daily, but hours vary from store to store. 921 SW Morrison St. (in the Galleria). ✆ **800/828-9673** or 503/241-3630.

www.madeinoregon.com. Also at Portland International Airport (① 503/ 282-7827); in Lloyd Center mall, SE Multnomah St. and SE Broadway (① 503/ 282-7636); and in Old Town at 10 NW First Ave. (① 503/273-8354).

JEWELRY

For some of the most creative jewelry in Portland, visit **Twist,** the **Graystone Gallery,** the **Hoffman Gallery,** the **Contemporary Crafts Gallery,** and the **Real Mother Goose.** See "Crafts," above.

MALLS & SHOPPING CENTERS

Lloyd Center   This large shopping mall in inner northeast Portland has five anchor stores and more than 200 specialty shops, including a Nordstrom and a Meier and Frank. A food court, ice-skating rink, and eight-screen cinema complete the mall's facilities. Bounded by SE Multnomah St., NE Broadway, NE 16th Ave., and NE Ninth Ave. ① 503/282-2511.

Pioneer Place   Just a block from Pioneer Courthouse Square, this is Portland's most upscale downtown shopping center. Anchored by a Saks Fifth Avenue, Pioneer Place is filled with stores selling designer fashions and expensive gifts. You'll also find the city's only Godiva chocolatier and Todai, a Japanese restaurant with a 160-foot sushi bar. 700 SW Fifth Ave. (between Third and Fifth aves.). ① 503/228-5800.

MARKETS

Portland Saturday Market   The Portland Saturday Market (held on both Sat and Sun) is arguably the city's single most important and best-loved event. For years the Northwest has attracted artists and craftspeople, and every Saturday and Sunday nearly 300 of them can be found selling their creations here. In addition to the dozens of crafts stalls, you'll find ethnic and unusual foods, and lots of free entertainment. This is one of the best places in Portland to shop for one-of-a-kind gifts. The atmosphere is always cheerful, and the crowds are always colorful. Don't miss it. On Sunday, on-street parking is free. Under the west end of the Burnside Bridge (between SW First Ave. and SW Naito Pkwy.). ① 503/222-6072. www.portlandsaturdaymarket.com. Open from the first weekend in March to Christmas Eve, Sat 10am–5pm, Sun 11am–4:30pm; closed Jan–Feb.

TOYS

Finnegan's Toys and Gifts   This is the largest toy store in downtown Portland. It'll have your inner child kicking and screaming if you don't buy that silly little toy you never got when you were young. 922 SW Yamhill St. ② **503/221-0306**. www.finneganstoys.com.

WINE

Oregon Wines on Broadway   This cozy wine bar/shop is located diagonally across from the Hotel Vintage Plaza in downtown Portland. Here you can taste some of Oregon's fine wines, including 30 different Pinot Noirs, as well as Chardonnays, Gewürztraminers and Washington state Cabernet Sauvignons and Merlots. 515 SW Broadway. ② **503/228-4655**.

9

Portland After Dark

Portland is the Northwest's number two cultural center (after Seattle, of course). The city's symphony orchestra, ballet, and opera are all well regarded, and the many theater companies offer classic and contemporary plays. If you're a jazz fan, you'll feel right at home—there's always a lot of live jazz being played around town. In summer, festivals move the city's cultural activities outdoors.

To find out what's going on during your visit, pick up a copy of *Willamette Week,* Portland's free weekly arts-and-entertainment newspaper. The *Oregonian,* the city's daily newspaper, also publishes lots of entertainment-related information in its Friday "A&E" section and also in the Sunday edition of the paper.

1 The Performing Arts

For the most part, the Portland performing-arts scene revolves around the **Portland Center for the Performing Arts (PCPA),** 1111 SW Broadway (② **503/248-4335**), which is comprised of five performances spaces in three different buildings. The **Arlene Schnitzer Concert Hall,** Southwest Broadway and Southwest Main Street, known locally as the Schnitz, is an immaculately restored 1920s movie palace that still displays the original Portland theater sign and marquee out front and is home to the Oregon Symphony. This hall also hosts popular music performers, lecturers, and many other special performances. Directly across Main Street from the Schnitz, at 1111 SW Broadway, is the sparkling glass jewel box known as the **New Theater Building.** This building houses both the **Newmark** and **Dolores Winningstad** theaters and **Brunish Hall.** The Newmark Theatre is home to Portland Center Stage, while the two theaters together host stage productions by local and visiting companies. Free tours of all three of these theaters are held Wednesdays at 11am, Saturdays every half hour between 11am and 1pm, and the first Thursday of every month at 6pm.

A few blocks away from this concentration of venues is the 3,000-seat **Keller Auditorium,** SW Third Avenue and SW Clay Street, the largest of the four halls and the home of the Portland Opera and the Oregon Ballet Theatre. The auditorium was constructed shortly after World War I and completely remodeled in the 1960s. In addition to the resident companies mentioned above, these halls host numerous visiting companies each year, including touring Broadway shows.

Note that PCPA's box office is open for ticket sales only for 2 hours before a show. At other times, tickets to PCPA performances and also performances at many other venues around the city, are sold through either **Ticketmaster** (© **503/224-4400;** www.ticket master.com), which has outlets at area G.I. Joe's and Meier and Frank stores, or **Fastixx** (© **800/992-TIXX** or 503/224-8499; www.fastixx.com), which has outlets at area Safeway stores. You can also purchase tickets to PCPA performances and other shows at **Ticket Central** (© **503/275-8358**), which is located at the **Portland Oregon Visitors Association (POVA) Information Center,** 701 SW Sixth Ave., Suite 1, in Pioneer Courthouse Square. This ticket office also sells day-of-show, half-price tickets to many area performances.

For much more daring and cutting edge performances, check out the calendar of the **Portland Institute for Contemporary Art (PICA),** 219 NW 12th Ave. (© **503/242-1419;** www.pica.org), which was created as a resource for exploring and supporting experimental art and new music in this city. PICA presents innovative performances by both well-known and less-established performance artists and musicians, as well as visual exhibitions focusing on contemporary trends in the regional, national, and international art scene. Call for a current schedule of performance events, which are held at various venues around town (tickets $16–$23).

One other performing arts venue worth checking out is **The Old Church,** 1422 SW 11th Ave. (© **503/222-2031;** www.oldchurch. org). Built in 1883, this wooden Carpenter Gothic church is a Portland landmark. It incorporates a grand traditional design, but was constructed with spare ornamentation. Today the building serves as a community facility, and every Wednesday at noon it hosts free lunchtime classical music concerts. There are also many other performances held here throughout the year.

OPERA & CLASSICAL MUSIC

Founded in 1896, the **Oregon Symphony** (© **800/228-7343** or 503/228-1353; www.orsymphony.org), which performs at the Arlene Schnitzer Concert Hall, 1111 SW Broadway (see above), is the oldest symphony orchestra on the West Coast. Under the expert baton of conductor James DePreist, the symphony has achieved national recognition and each year between September and June stages several series, including classical, pops, Sunday matinees, and children's concerts. Ticket prices range from $15 to $55 (seniors and students may purchase half-price tickets 1 hr. before a classical or pops concert; Mon nights there are $5 student tickets).

Each season, the **Portland Opera** (© 503/241-1802; www. portlandopera.org), which performs at Keller Auditorium, SW Third Avenue and SW Clay Street (see above), offers five different productions that include both grand opera and light opera. The season runs September through May. Ticket prices range from $25 to $155.

Summer is the time for Portland's annual chamber music binge. **Chamber Music Northwest** (© 503/294-6400; www.cmnw.org) is a 5-week-long series that starts in late June and attracts the world's finest chamber musicians. Performances are held at Reed College and Catlin Gable School (tickets $17–$33).

THEATER

Portland Center Stage (© 503/274-6588; www.pcs.org), which holds performances at the Portland Center for the Performing Arts, 1111 SW Broadway (see above), is Portland's largest professional theater company. They stage a combination of six classic and contemporary plays during their September-to-April season (tickets $16–$44).

The play's the thing at **Tygres Heart Shakespeare Co.** (© 503/ 288-8400; www.tygresheart.org), which performs at the Dolores Winningstad Theatre, 1111 SW Broadway (see above), and old Will would be proud. Tygres Heart remains true to its name and stages only works by the Bard himself. The three-play season runs September through May (tickets $11–$32).

If it's musicals you want, you've got a couple of options in Portland. At the Keller Auditorium, you can catch the **Portland Opera Presents the Best of Broadway** series (© 503/241-1802; www.broadwayseries.com). Tickets range from around $15 to $69. For other Broadway classics, check the schedule of the **Musical Theatre Company** (© 503/916-6592 or 503/224-5411; www.the musicaltheatrecompany.com), a semiprofessional company that performs at the Eastside Performance Center, SE 14th Avenue and SE Stark Street. The season runs September through May (tickets $26–$30 for adults, $24–$28 for seniors, and $16 for students).

DANCE

Although the **Oregon Ballet Theatre** (© **888/922-5538** or 503/222-5538; www.obt.org), which performs at the Keller Auditorium and the Newmark Theatre (see above), is best loved for its sold-out performances each December of *The Nutcracker,* this company also stages the annual American Choreographers Showcase. This latter performance often features world premieres. Rounding out the season are performances of classic and contemporary ballets (tickets $5–$80).

PERFORMING ARTS SERIES

The **Museum After Hours** series at the **Portland Art Museum's North Wing,** 1119 SW Park Ave. (© **503/226-2811**), is a great place to catch some of the best local jazz, blues, rock, and folk bands. Performances are held October through April on Wednesday nights from 5:30 to 7:30pm, and admission is $6.

When summer hits, Portlanders like to head outdoors to hear music. The city's top outdoor music series is held at **Washington Park Zoo,** 4001 SW Canyon Rd. (© **503/226-1561;** www.oregonzoo.org), which brings in the likes of Bonnie Raitt, John Prine, and Leo Kottke.

2 The Club & Music Scene

ROCK, BLUES & FOLK

Aladdin Theater   This former movie theater now serves as one of Portland's main venues for touring performers such as Richard Thompson, the Buena Vista Social Club, and Brian Wilson. The very diverse musical spectrum represented includes blues, rock, ethnic, country, folk, and jazz. There are also regular singer-songwriter programs. 3017 SE Milwaukie Ave. © **503/233-1994.** www.showman.com. Tickets $10–$25.

Berbati's Pan   Located in Old Town, this is currently one of Portland's most popular rock clubs. A wide variety of acts play here, primarily the best of the local rock scene and bands on the verge of breaking into the national limelight. 231 SW Ankeny St. © **503/248-4579.** www.berbati.citysearch.com. Cover $5–$15.

Crystal Ballroom   The Crystal Ballroom first opened before 1920, and since then has seen performers ranging from early jazz musicians to James Brown, Marvin Gaye, and the Grateful Dead. The McMenamin Brothers (of local brewing fame) renovated the Crystal Ballroom several years back and refurbished its dance floor, which, due to its mechanics, feels as if it's floating. The ballroom now hosts a variety of performances and special events nearly every night of the week. **Lola's Room,** a smaller version of the Ballroom, is on the second floor and also has a floating dance floor. You'll find **Ringlers Pub** (a colorful brewpub) on the ground floor. 1332 W. Burnside St. ⓒ 503/225-0047 ext. 239 for box office, 503/225-5555 ext. 8811 for concert information. www.danceonair.com. Cover free–$28.

Roseland Theater & Grill   The Roseland Theater, though it isn't all that large, is currently Portland's premier live music club for touring national name acts. You might encounter the likes of the Neville Brothers, Tower of Power, or Steel Pulse. There's also a restaurant affiliated with the club. 8 NW Sixth Ave. ⓒ 503/219-9929. Cover $5–$35.

JAZZ

Jazz De Opus   Located in the Old Town nightlife district, this restaurant/bar has long been one of Portland's bastions of jazz, with a cozy room and smooth sounds on the stereo. You can also catch live performances nightly by jazz musicians. 33 NW Second Ave. ⓒ 503/222-6077. Cover $5 on weekends.

The Lobby Court   Hands down the most elegant old-world bar in Portland, the Lobby Court is in the city's most luxurious hotel. The Circassian walnut paneling and crystal chandeliers will definitely put you in the mood for a martini or single malt. Tuesday through Saturday, there's live jazz in the evening. In the Benson Hotel, 309 SW Broadway. ⓒ 503/228-2000.

Typhoon! Imperial Lounge   Located off the lobby of downtown Portland's Imperial Hotel, this bar has live jazz Thursday through Saturday nights. Big windows fronting on the sidewalk let you check out the scene before venturing in. An eclectic array of musicians makes this place a bit different from other area jazz clubs. In the Imperial Hotel, 400 SW Broadway. ⓒ 503/224-8285. No cover.

CABARET

Darcelle's XV   In business since 1967 and run by Portland's best-loved cross-dresser, this cabaret is a campy Portland institution with a female-impersonator show that has been a huge hit for years. There are shows Wednesday through Saturday. 208 NW Third Ave. ⓒ 503/222-5338. www.darcellexv.citysearch.com. Cover $10. Reservations recommended.

DANCE CLUBS

See also the listing for Saucebox, below, under "Bars"; this restaurant and bar becomes a dance club after 10pm, when a DJ begins spinning tunes.

Andrea's Cha-Cha Club   Located in the Grand Cafe and open on Wednesday through Saturday nights, this is Portland's premier dance spot for fans of Latin dancing. Whether it's cha-cha, salsa, or the latest dance craze from south of the border, they'll be doing it here. Lessons are available between 8:30 and 9:30pm. 832 SE Grand Ave. ℂ 503/230-1166. Cover $1–$3.

Bar 71   Located in the Old Town nightlife district, Bar 71 is a mixed-use sort of place. It offers DJ dancing Thursday through Saturday on the back patio, pool tables in front, and good bar food. It's the classiest of the Old Town bars. In summer, you can dance under the stars. 71 SW Second Ave. ℂ 503/241-0938. No cover before 9:30pm, $5 9:30–10pm, $10 after 10pm.

3 The Bar & Pub Scene

BARS

The Brazen Bean   What started out as a late-night coffeehouse is now a very hip cocktail and cigar bar with a fin-de-siècle European elegance in Northwest Portland. This is mainly a man's domain, but cigar-puffing women will appreciate it as well. 2075 NW Glisan St. ℂ 503/294-0636.

Jake's Famous Crawfish   In business since 1892, Jake's is a Portland institution and should not be missed (see the full review on p. 63). The bar is one of the busiest in town when the downtown offices let out. 401 SW 12th Ave. ℂ 503/226-1419.

McCormick and Schmick's Harborside Pilsner Room
Located at the south end of Tom McCall Waterfront Park overlooking the Willamette River and RiverPlace Marina, this restaurant/bar is affiliated with Hood River's Full Sail brewery and keeps 10 Full Sail brews on tap (plus 15 other area beers). The crowd is upscale, the view one of the best in town. (See p. 63 for a review of the restaurant.) 0309 SW Montgomery St. ℂ 503/220-1865. www.mccormickand schmicks.com.

Öba!   Currently one of the trendiest bars in Portland, this big Pearl District bar/nuevo Latino restaurant has a very tropical feel despite the warehouse district locale. After work, the bar is always

Portland's Brewing Up a Microstorm

Espresso may be the drink that drives Portland, but when it's time to relax and kick back, **microbrewed beer** is often the beverage of choice around these parts. No other city in America has as large a concentration of brewpubs, and it was here that the craft brewing business got its start in the mid-1980s. Today, brewpubs can be found throughout the city, with cozy neighborhood pubs vying for business with big, polished establishments.

To fully appreciate what the city's craft brewers are concocting, it helps to have a little beer background. Beer has **four basic ingredients:** malt, hops, yeast, and water. The first of these, **malt,** is made from grains, primarily barley and wheat, which are roasted to convert their carbohydrates into the sugar needed to grow yeast. The amount of roasting the grains receive during the malting process determines the color and flavor of the final product. The darker the malt, the darker and more flavorful the beer or ale. There is a wide variety of malts, each providing its own characteristic flavor. **Yeast,** in turn, converts the malt's sugar into alcohol; there are many different strains of yeast that all lend different characters to beers. The **hops** are added to give beer its characteristic bitterness. The more "hoppy" the beer or ale, the more bitter it becomes. The Northwest is the nation's only commercial hop-growing region, with 75% grown in Washington and 25% grown in Oregon and Idaho.

Lagers, which are cold-fermented, are the most common beers in America and are made from pale malt with a lot of

packed with the stylish and the upwardly mobile. Don't miss the tropical-fruit margaritas! 555 NW 12th Ave. ✆ 503/228-6161.

Paragon   Dark and cavernous, this Pearl District warehouse makeover is among the hippest hangouts in town, and regulars like to dress to impress. Not so overdone that you can't recognize the space's industrial heritage, this place has a sort of Edward-Hopper-meets-the-21st-century feel. There's live music on Wednesday and Thursday nights and a DJ on Fridays and Saturdays. 1309 NW Hoyt St. ✆ 503/833-5060. www.paragonrestaurant.com.

hops added to give them their characteristic bitter flavor. **Pilsner**, a style of beer that originated in the mid–19th century in Czechoslovakia, is a type of lager. **Ales**, which are the most common brews served at microbreweries, are made using a warm fermentation process and usually with more and darker malt than is used in lagers and pilsners. **Porters** and **stouts** get their characteristic dark coloring and flavor from the use of dark, even charred, malt.

To these basics, you can then add a few variables. **Fruit-flavored beers**, which some disparage as soda-pop beer, are actually an old European tradition and, when considering the abundance of fresh fruits in the Northwest, are a natural here. Also immensely popular in Portland are **hefe-weizens** (German-style wheat beers), which have a cloudy appearance, and IPAs (**Indian pale ales**), which are strong and hoppy. If you see a sign for **nitro beer** in a pub, it isn't referring to their explosive brews—it means they've got a keg charged with nitrogen instead of carbon dioxide. The nitrogen gives the beer an extra creamy head. (A nitro charge is what makes Guinness Stout so distinctive.) **Cask-conditioned ales**, served almost room temperature and with only their own carbon dioxide to create the head, are also gaining in popularity. Although some people find these brews flat, others appreciate them for their unadulterated character.

It all adds up to a lot of variety in Portland pubs. Cheers!

Saucebox   Popular with the city's scene-makers, this downtown hybrid restaurant-bar is a large, dramatically lit dark box that can be very noisy. If you want to talk, you'd better do it before 10pm, when the DJ arrives to transform this place from restaurant into dance club. Great cocktails. 214 SW Broadway. ℭ 503/241-3393.

WINE BARS
Oregon Wines on Broadway   With just a handful of stools at the bar and a couple of cozy tables, this tiny place is the best spot in Portland to learn about Oregon wines. On any given night there

will be 30 Oregon Pinot Noirs available by the glass, and plenty of white wines as well. 515 SW Broadway. ⓒ 503/228-4655.

Southpark Seafood Grill & Wine Bar   With its high ceiling, long heavy drapes, halogen lights, and lively wall mural, the wine bar at Southpark (see the full dining review on p. 64) is a contemporary interpretation of a Parisian cafe from the turn of the last century. Very romantic. 901 SW Salmon St. ⓒ 503/326-1300.

BREWPUBS

They're brewing beers in Portland the likes of which you won't taste in too many other places on this side of the Atlantic. This is the heart of the Northwest craft-brewing explosion, and if you're a beer connoisseur, you owe it to yourself to go directly to the source.

Brewpubs have become big business in Portland, and there are now glitzy upscale pubs as well as funky warehouse-district locals. No matter what vision you have of the ideal brewpub, you're likely to find your dream come true. Whether you're wearing bike shorts or a three-piece suit, there's a pub in Portland where you can enjoy a handcrafted beer, a light meal, and a convivial atmosphere.

With almost three dozen brewpubs in the Portland metropolitan area, the McMenamins chain is Portland's biggest brewpub empire. The owners of this empire think of themselves as court jesters, mixing brewing fanaticism with a Deadhead aesthetic. Throw in a bit of historic preservation and a strong belief in family-friendly neighborhood pubs and you'll understand why these joints are so popular.

DOWNTOWN

McMenamins Ringlers Pub   With mosaic pillars framing the bar, Indonesian antiques, and big old signs all around, this cavernous place is about as eclectic a brewpub as you'll ever find. A block away are two associated pubs in a flat-iron building; one is below street level with a beer cellar feel and the other has walls of multipaned glass. These three pubs are the most atmospheric alehouses in town. 1332 W. Burnside St. ⓒ 503/225-0627. www.mcmenamins.com.

Tugboat Brewpub   This tiny brewpub on an alley-like street just off Broadway near The Benson hotel is just what a good local pub should be. With its picnic-table decor, it's decidedly casual, but the shelves of books lend the place a literary bent. Good brews, too. 711 SW Ankeny St. ⓒ 503/226-2508.

NORTHWEST PORTLAND

BridgePort Brewery and BrewPub   Located in the trendy Pearl District, Portland's oldest microbrewery was founded in 1984 and is housed in the city's oldest industrial building (where workers once produced rope for sailing ships). The ivy-draped old brick building has loads of character, just right for enjoying craft ales, of which there are usually four to seven on tap on any given night (including several cask-conditioned ales). The pub also makes great pizza. 1313 NW Marshall St. ℂ 888/834-7546 or 503/241-7179. www. bridgeportbrew.com.

Portland Brewing Company's Brewhouse Tap Room and Grill   With huge copper fermenting vats proudly displayed and polished to a high sheen, this is by far the city's most ostentatious, though certainly not its largest, brewpub. We aren't particularly fond of the brews here, but Portland Brewing's MacTarnahan's Scottish-style amber ale does have some very loyal fans. 2730 NW 31st Ave. ℂ 503/228-5269.

Rogue Ales Public House   This Pearl District pub is an outpost of a popular microbrewery headquartered in the Oregon coast community of Newport. Rogue produces just about the widest variety of beers in the state, and, best of all, keeps lots of them on tap at this pub. If you're a fan of barley-wine ale, don't miss their Old Crustacean. 1339 NW Flanders St. ℂ 503/241-3800.

SOUTHEAST

The Lucky Labrador Brew Pub   With a warehouse-size room, industrial feel, and picnic tables on the loading dock out back, this brewpub is a classic southeast Portland local. The crowd is young, and dogs are welcome. (They don't even have to be Labs.) 915 SE Hawthorne Blvd. ℂ 503/236-3555. www.luckylab.com.

NORTHEAST & NORTH PORTLAND

Alameda Brewhouse   With its industrial chic interior, this high-ceilinged neighborhood pub brews up some of the most unusual beers in Portland. How about a rose-petal bock, a juniper-berry porter, or a heather-flower ale made without hops? Some work, some don't, but fans of craft beers have to appreciate the willingness to experiment. 4765 NE Fremont St. ℂ 503/460-9025.

McMenamins Kennedy School   Never thought they'd ever start serving beer in elementary school, did you? However, in the hands of the local McMenamins brewpub empire, an old northeast

---

Moments A Portland Original: The Theater Pub

Portland brewpub magnates the McMenamin brothers have a novel way to sell their craft ales—in movie pubs. Although it's often hard to concentrate on the screen, it's always a lot of fun to attend a show. The movies are usually recent releases that have played the main theaters but have not yet made it onto video. Theaters include the **Bagdad Theater,** 3702 SE Hawthorne Blvd. (© **503/236-9234**), a restored classic Arabian Nights movie palace; the **Mission Theater,** 1624 NW Glisan St. (© **503/223-4527**), which was the first McMenamins theater pub; the **Kennedy School Theater,** 5736 NE 33rd Ave. (© **503/288-2192**), in a former elementary school; and the **Edgefield Theater,** 2126 SW Halsey St., Troutdale (© **503/ 492-4686**).

Portland school has been transformed into a sprawling complex complete with brewpub, beer garden, movie theater pub, a cigar-and-cocktails room, even a bed-and-breakfast inn. Order up a pint and wander the halls checking out all the cool artwork. 5736 NE 33rd Ave. © 503/288-2192. www.mcmenamins.com.

Widmer Brewing and Gasthaus   Located in an industrial area just north of the Rose Garden arena, this place has the feel of a classic blue-collar pub. This is the brewery for Portland's largest craft brewing company, which is best known for its hefe-weizen. German and American foods are served. 955 N. Russell St. © 503/281-3333. www.widmer.com.

4 The Gay & Lesbian Nightlife Scene

A DANCE CLUB

Embers Avenue   Though primarily a gay disco, Embers is also popular with straights. There are always lots of flashing lights and sweaty bodies until the early morning. Look for drag shows 6 nights a week; on Mondays, movies are shown on a giant-screen TV. 110 NW Broadway. © 503/222-3082. Cover Fri–Sat $5, Sun–Thurs free.

BARS

The area around the intersection of **SW Stark Street and West Burnside Street** has the largest concentration of gay bars in Portland.

Eagle PDX   If leather and Levi's are your uniform, then you'll feel right at home in this dive bar. Loud rock music plays in the background, and it's popular with a young crowd. Long happy hours with good prices. 1300 W. Burnside St. © 503/241-0105.

Scandal's & The Otherside Lounge   In business for more than 20 years, this bar/restaurant is at the center of the gay bar scene. There always seems to be some special event going on here. 1038 SW Stark St. © 503/227-5887. www.scandals.citysearch.com.

10

Side Trips from Portland

Portland likes to boast about how close it is to both mountains and ocean, and no visit would be complete without a trip or two to salt-water or snow. In 1½ hours you can be walking on a Pacific Ocean beach or skiing in the Cascade Range—even in the middle of summer, when there is lift-accessed snow skiing on Mount Hood. A drive through the Columbia River Gorge, a National Scenic Area, is an absolute must; and if wine is your interest, you can spend a day visiting wineries and driving through the rolling farmland that enticed pioneers to travel the Oregon Trail beginning in the 1840s.

1 The Columbia Gorge & Mount Hood Loop

If you have time for only one excursion from Portland, I strongly urge you to do the Mount Hood Loop. This is a long trip, so start your day as early as possible.

To begin your trip, take I-84 east out of Portland. At Troutdale, take the exit marked **Historic Columbia River Highway** (U.S. 30) ↛↛, which was built between 1913 and 1922. The highway was an engineering marvel in its day, but it is dwarfed by the spectacular vistas that present themselves whenever the scenic road emerges from the dark forest. To learn more about the road and how it was built, stop at **Vista House** ↛↛, 733 feet above the river on **Crown Point.** There are informative displays with old photos and a spectacular view of the gorge, including **Beacon Rock** ↛↛, an 800-foot-tall monolith on the far side of the river.

Between Troutdale and Ainsworth State Park, 22 miles east, you'll pass numerous waterfalls, including Latourelle, Shepherds Dell, Bridal Veil, Wahkeena, Horsetail, Oneonta, and **Multnomah Falls** ↛↛↛. At 620 feet from lip to pool, Multnomah Falls is the tallest waterfall in Oregon and is one of the state's top tourist attractions. Expect crowds. A paved trail leads from the base of the falls to the top and connects with other unpaved trails that are usually not at all crowded.

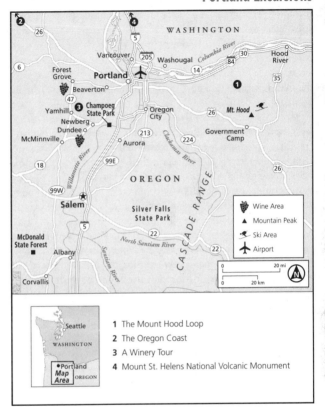

1 The Mount Hood Loop
2 The Oregon Coast
3 A Winery Tour
4 Mount St. Helens National Volcanic Monument

Not far beyond Multnomah Falls, you'll come to the narrow **Oneonta Gorge** 🌂🌂. This narrow cleft in the rock has long been a popular summertime walk for the sure of foot. The gorge can usually be explored for about half a mile upstream to a waterfall that pours into a small pool of very cold water. There is no trail here; you just hike up the creek itself, so wear shoes that can get wet. Due to an unstable logjam at the mouth of Oneonta Gorge, the Forest Service has been discouraging people from hiking into this little gorge. Enter at your own risk.

The next stop on your tour should be **Bonneville Lock and Dam** 🌂. One of the dam's most important features, attracting thousands of visitors each year, is its fish ladder, which allows the upriver migration of salmon and other *anadromous* fish (fish that are spawned in freshwater, mature in saltwater, and return to freshwater to spawn). Underwater windows permit visitors to see fish as they pass through the ladder. Visit the adjacent fish hatchery to see how trout, salmon, and sturgeon are raised before they are released into the river. June and September are the best months to observe salmon at the fish ladder.

This is the first of many dams on the Columbia River and, along with the other dams, is currently the focus of a heated environmental debate over saving the region's dwindling native wild salmon populations. Despite fish ladders and fish hatcheries, wild salmon have been fighting an upstream battle for survival. Adult salmon heading upstream to spawn have to contend with fishermen (both commercial and sport), and spawning beds that are sometimes destroyed or silted up, often by the common practice of clear-cutting timber from steep mountainsides. Among the perils faced by young salmon heading downstream are slow, warm waters that delay the journey to the Pacific Ocean, electrical turbines in dams (these kill countless numbers of fish), and irrigation culverts that often lead salmon out into farm fields. With many populations now listed as threatened species (one step below endangered species), a plan for salmon survival is being hammered out. It is hoped that the dams that once brought prosperity and cheap electricity to the Northwest won't bring about the demise of the salmon.

Not far past the dam is the **Bridge of the Gods,** a two-lane toll bridge that connects Oregon to Washington at the site where an Indian legend says a natural bridge once stood. Geologists are now convinced that this legend has its basis in a relatively recent geological event—a massive landslide that may have occurred as recently as 250 years ago. The slide completely blocked the river, and when the Columbia finally poured over the top of this natural dam, the water unleashed a 100-foot flood downstream and rapidly eroded the natural earthen dam leaving only huge slabs of rocks in the riverbed. These rocks created the Cascades for which both the Cascade Range and Cascade Locks were named.

On the Washington side of the Columbia River, east of the Bridge of the Gods, is the **Columbia Gorge Interpretive Center** ★★, 990 SW Rock Creek Dr., Stevenson (© **800/991-2338;** www. columbiagorge.org). This modern museum is the single best introduction to the natural and human history of the Columbia Gorge and has an awesome view (when it's not cloudy). Exhibits focus on

The Columbia Gorge & Mount Hood Loop

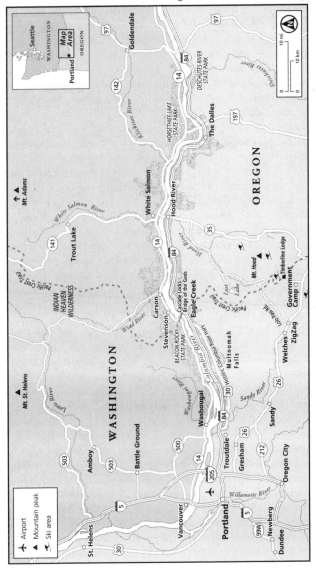

the Gorge's early Native-American inhabitants and the development of the area by white settlers. A relic here that you can't miss is a 37-foot-high replica of a 19th-century fish wheel, which helps show how salmon runs were decimated in the past. Admission is $6 for adults, $5 for seniors and students, $4 for children 6 to 12, and free for children under 6. The center is open daily from 10am to 5pm.

Just beyond Bridge of the Gods on the Oregon side are the **Cascade Locks.** These navigational locks were built to enable river traffic to avoid the treacherous passage through the cascades that once existed at this spot. In earlier years, many boats were portaged around the cascades instead of attempting the dangerous trip. When the locks were opened in 1896, they made traveling between The Dalles and Portland much easier. But the completion of the Historic Columbia River Highway in 1922 made the trip even easier by land. With the construction of the Bonneville Dam, the cascades were flooded, and the locks became superfluous.

There are two small museums here at the locks, one of which also holds the ticket office for the **Sternwheeler *Columbia Gorge*** (© **800/643-1354,** 503/223-3928 in Portland, or 541/374-8427 in Cascade Locks), which makes regular trips on the river between mid-June and late September. These boat tours provide a fascinating glimpse of the Columbia Gorge and are highly recommended. Tours, which last 2 hours, cost $14.95 for adults and $8.95 for children.

Anyone who boardsails has likely heard of the town of **Hood River**. This section of the Columbia River is one of the most popular boardsailing spots in the world because of the strong winds that blow through the gorge in summer. Almost every other car in this once-sleepy little town seems to have a sailboard on the roof. If you want to try this sport yourself, stop by one of the many sailboard shops downtown for information on rentals and lessons.

If you are staying overnight on the loop, you might want to consider getting out of your car and riding the rails. The **Mount Hood Railroad**, 110 Railroad Ave., Hood River (© **800/872-4661**), operates an excursion train from late March to late December carrying passengers up the Hood River Valley from the town of Hood River to Parkdale and back. The railroad cars are vintage Pullman coaches, and the Mount Hood Railroad Depot is a National Historic Site. The excursions last 4 hours, and fares are $22.95 for adults, $20.95 for seniors, and $14.95 for children 2 to 12. The schedule varies with the season, so call ahead to make a reservation. There are also regularly scheduled dinner, brunch, and other specialty excursions. Mid-April's Fruit Blossom Express runs when the fruit orchards are in bloom, and in mid-October, there are Harvest Festival excursions.

From Hood River, turn south on Oregon Hwy. 35, passing through thousands of acres of apple and pear orchards. Every fall, roadside stands in this area sell fresh fruit and fruit products. The orchards are especially beautiful in the spring, when the trees are in bloom. No matter what time of year, you will have the snow-covered peak of Mount Hood in view as you drive through the orchards, making them all the more spectacular.

Just after Hwy. 35 merges into U.S. 26, turn right onto the road to **Timberline Lodge** 🌟🌟. As the name implies, this lodge is at the timberline, and a July or August walk on one of the trails in the vicinity will lead you through wildflower-filled meadows. Surprisingly, because of the glacier and snowfields above the lodge, you can also ski and snowboard here all summer long.

Between Government Camp and the community of Zig Zag, watch for the roadside marker that marks the western end of the **Barlow Trail** toll road, a section of the Oregon Trail that circled around Mount Hood in order to avoid the dangerous downriver journey through the cascades of the Columbia River. There is a reproduction of the gate that once stood on this spot, and you can still see the trail itself, which is now open only to hikers, mountain bikers, and horseback riders.

To return to Portland just stay on Oregon Hwy. 26 all the way back to town or follow the signs for I-84.

WHERE TO STAY

Columbia Gorge Hotel 🌟🌟   Located just west of the town of Hood River off I-84 and opened shortly after the Columbia River Scenic Highway was completed in 1915, this little oasis of luxury offers the same genteel atmosphere that was once enjoyed by the likes of Rudolph Valentino and Clark Gable. With its yellow-stucco walls and red-tile roofs, this hotel would be right at home in Beverly Hills, and the hotel gardens could hold their own in Victoria, British Columbia. Despite the attractive furnishings and gardens, it is almost impossible to notice anything but the view from the windows. The hotel is perched more than 200 feet above the river on a steep cliff.

Guest rooms are all a little different, with a mixture of antique and classic furnishings. There are canopy beds, brass beds, and even some hand-carved wooden beds. Unfortunately, many of the rooms are rather cramped, as are the bathrooms, most of which have older fixtures. However, some rooms have soaking tubs and fireplaces.

4000 Westcliff Dr., Hood River, OR 97031. © 800/345-1921 or 541/386-5566. Fax 541/387-5414. www.columbiagorgehotel.com. 39 units. $169–$279 double. Rates include multicourse breakfast. AE, DC, DISC, MC, V. Pets accepted with $25 fee. **Amenities:** Restaurant (Northwest/Continental), lounge; concierge; room service; massage. In room: A/C, TV, dataport, hair dryer, iron, safe.

Dolce Skamania Lodge 🐸🐸🐸 Boasting the most spectacular vistas of any hotel in the Gorge, Skamania Lodge is also the only golf resort in the area. Although golf is the preferred sport here, the hotel is well situated whether you brought your sailboard, hiking boots, or mountain bike. The interior decor is classically rustic, with lots of rock and natural wood, and throughout the hotel there are Northwest Indian artworks and artifacts on display. Huge windows in the lobby take in a superb view of the Gorge. Of course, the river-view guest rooms are more expensive than the forest-view rooms (which overlook more parking lot than forest), but these rooms are well worth the extra cost. There are also rooms with fireplaces available. The lodge was planning to add 59 new rooms in late 2001, so you might want to request one of these new units.

P.O. Box 189, Stevenson, WA 98648. © 800/221-7117 or 509/427-7700. www.dolce.com/skamania. 253 units. $169–$199 double; $239–$385 suite. Lower rates in winter. AE, DC, DISC, MC, V. **Amenities:** Restaurant (Northwest), lounge; indoor pool; 18-hole golf course; 2 tennis courts; exercise room; Jacuzzi; sauna; bike rentals; children's programs; activities desk; business center; babysitting; room service; massage; laundry service. In room: A/C, TV, dataport, minibar, coffeemaker, hair dryer, iron.

Timberline Lodge 🐸🐸 Constructed during the Great Depression of the 1930s as a WPA project, this classic alpine ski lodge overflows with craftsmanship. The grand stone fireplace, huge exposed beams, and wide plank floors of the lobby impress every first-time visitor. Details are not overlooked either. Woodcarvings, imaginative wrought-iron fixtures, hand-hooked rugs, and hand-made furniture complete the rustic picture. Rooms vary in size considerably, with the smallest rooms lacking private bathrooms. However, no matter which unit you stay in, you'll be surrounded by the same rustic furnishings. Unfortunately, room windows are not very large, but you can always retire to the Ram's Head lounge for a better view of Mount Hood.

Timberline, OR 97028. (*C*) **800/547-1406** or 503/622-7979. Fax 503/622-0710. www.timberlinelodge.com. 70 units, 10 without private bathroom. $75 double with shared bathroom, $115–$225 double with private bathroom. AE, DISC, MC, V. Sno-park permit required in winter, but hotel will provide guests with one. **Amenities:** 2 restaurants (Northwest/American), 2 lounges; small outdoor pool; Jacuzzi; sauna; children's ski programs; coin-op laundry. *In room:* TV, dataport, hair dryer, iron, safe.

2 The Northern Oregon Coast

One of the most beautiful coastlines in the United States, the spectacular Oregon coast is this state's main tourist destination and is offers countless summer vacation spots along its length. The beach is less than 2 hours away from Portland and offers everything from rugged coves to long sandy beaches, artists' communities to classic family beach towns.

The quickest route from Portland to the Oregon coast (80 miles) is via U.S. 26, also called the **Sunset Highway.** Outlined here is a driving tour that takes in the very best of the northern Oregon coast. It's a long day's drive, so be sure to get an early start.

Just before reaching the coast and the junction with U.S. 101, watch for a sign for the **world's largest Sitka spruce tree.** This giant, more than 750 years old, is located in a small park just off the highway. Trees of this size were once common throughout the Coast Range, but almost all have now been cut down. The fight to preserve the remaining big trees is a bitter one that has divided the citizens of Oregon.

If you've got kids with you, turn north at the junction with U.S. 101 and head into **Seaside,** the coast's most traditional beach town (beachside promenade, saltwater taffy, arcade games, the works).

Otherwise, head south and watch for the turnoff to **Cannon Beach** *ᏮᏮᏮ*, the artsiest little town on the Oregon coast. Cannon Beach, though quite touristy, still has so much charm, you'll likely start scheming a way to retire here yourself.

Located just north of the town of Cannon Beach is **Ecola Beach State Park** *ᏮᏮ* ((*C*) **800/551-6949** or 503/436-2844), which provides some of the most spectacular views on the coast. Here in the park, there are stands of old-growth spruce, hemlock, and Douglas fir, and several trails offer a chance to walk through this lush forest. The park's Indian Beach is popular with surfers. For great views to the south, head to the Ecola Point picnic area, which is to your left just after you enter the park. A relatively easy 3-mile round-trip hiking trail connects this picnic area with Indian Beach.

Cannon Beach was named for a cannon off the USS *Shark,* which washed ashore here after that ship sank in 1849. Just offshore from the south end of town is **Haystack Rock** 🟊🟊, a massive 235-foot-tall island that is the most photographed rock on the coast. Only a few feet out from the beach, it's a popular destination of beach-combers and tide-pool explorers. In town, there are many art galleries and interesting shops.

Every summer, in early June, Cannon Beach celebrates **Sandcastle Day,** a festival that attracts numerous sand sculptors and thousands of appreciative viewers. Any time of year you'll find the winds here ideal for kite flying. However, forget about doing any swimming; the waters here, and all along the Oregon coast are too cold and rough for swimming.

Heading south out of Cannon Beach on U.S. 101, watch for the **Arcadia Beach State Recreation Site** 🟊🟊. This is one of the prettiest little beaches in the area, with haystack rocks and a headland that blocks the northwest winds in the summer months.

A little farther south, you'll come to **Hug Point State Recreation Site** 🟊🟊, with more headland-framed beach. Here you can also see an old stretch of the original coast highway. Although the old highway was mostly just the beach, here at Hug Point, the road was blasted into a headland, thus hugging the point.

A little farther south you'll come to the rugged **Oswald West State Park** 🟊🟊 (ⓒ **800/551-6949** or 503/436-2844), named for the governor who promoted legislation to preserve all Oregon beaches as public property. The beach is in a cove that can only be reached by walking a few hundred yards through dense forest; once you're there, all you'll hear is the crashing of the surf. The beach is strewn with huge driftwood logs that give it a wild look. High bluffs rise up at both ends of the cove and it is possible to hike to the top of them. There are plenty of picnic tables and a walk-in campground. This is another popular surfing spot.

U.S. 101 continues south from Oswald West State Park and climbs up over **Neahkahnie Mountain** 🟊. Legend has it that at the base of this ocean-side mountain, the survivors of a wrecked Spanish galleon buried a fortune in gold. Keep your eyes open for elk, which frequently graze in the meadows here.

Just below this windswept mountain is the quiet beach town of **Manzanita** 🟊🟊. Tucked under the fir, spruce, and hemlock trees are attractive summer homes. With Neahkahnie Mountain rising to the north, a long stretch of sandy beach fronting the town, and a

The Northern Oregon Coast

▲ Campground
▲ Mountain peak

WASHINGTON

Fort Stevens S.P. ▲ ■
Columbia River
Warrenton ○
Astoria ●
Lewis and Clark N.W.R. ■
101
30
To Portland →

Gearhart ○
Seaside ●
Tillamook Head
Ecola S.P. ■
Cannon Beach ○
Haystack Rock ■
Arcadia State Wayside ■
Hug Point S.P. ■
Arch Cape ○
Oswald West S.P. ■ ▲
Manzanita ○
Nehalem Bay S.P. ■
Nehalem Bay
Rockaway Beach ○
Garibaldi ●
Tillamook Bay
Cape Meares ■
Cape Meares S.P. ■
Oceanside ●
Netarts Bay
Cape Lookout S.P. ■
▲
Cape Lookout
Tierra Del Mar ○
Cape Kiwanda S.P. ■
Cape Kiwanda
Woods ○
Nestucca Bay
Pacific City ○

Saddle Mtn. S.P. ■ ▲ Saddle Mtn.
World's largest Sitka spruce ■
Elsie ○
26
53
To Portland →
Klaskanine River
Nehalem River
Wilson River
To Portland →
Bay City ●
6
Trask River
Tillamook ●
Beaver ○
SIUSLAW NATIONAL FOREST
COAST RANGES

PACIFIC OCEAN

Seattle ●
WASHINGTON
Map Area
Portland ●
OREGON

0 ___ 10 mi
0 ___ 10 km
N

Nehalem Bay State Park ⨍ (ⓒ **800/551-6949** or 503/368-5154) to the south of town, Manzanita is one of our favorite Oregon beach towns.

Tillamook Bay is one of the largest bays on the Oregon coast and at its north end is the small town of **Garibaldi,** which is a popular sportfishing spot. If you aren't an angler, you can still go for a cruise either around the bay or to look for whales.

Two miles north of the busy farm town of **Tillamook** on U.S. 101, you will come to the **Tillamook Cheese Factory** ⨍ (ⓒ **503/815-1300;** www.tillamookcheese.com). This region is one of Oregon's main dairy-farming areas, and much of the milk is turned into cheddar cheese and butter. Today this is one of the most popular attractions on the Oregon coast, and you can watch the cheese-making process through large windows. The cheese-factory store is a busy place (especially the ice cream counter), but the lines move quickly and you can be on your way to the next picnic area with an assortment of tasty cheeses.

From Tillamook the **Three Capes Scenic Route** ★★ leads to Cape Meares, Cape Lookout, and Cape Kiwanda, all of which provide stunning vistas of rocky cliffs, misty mountains, and booming surf. As the name implies, this is a very scenic stretch of road, and there are plenty of places to stop and enjoy the views and the beaches.

Cape Meares State Scenic Viewpoint ★ perches high atop the cape, with the Cape Meares lighthouse just a short walk from the parking lot. This lighthouse, 200 feet above the water, was built in 1890. Today it has been replaced by an automated light a few feet away. Be sure to visit the **octopus tree** here in the park. This Sitka spruce has been twisted and sculpted by harsh weather.

As you come down from the cape, you'll reach the village of **Oceanside** ★, which clings to the steep mountainsides of a small cove. One tavern, one restaurant, and one cafe are the only commercial establishments, and that's the way folks here like it. If you walk north along the beach, you'll find a pedestrian tunnel through the headland that protects this hillside community. Through the tunnel is another beautiful stretch of beach.

South of Oceanside, the road runs along a flat stretch of beach before reaching **Cape Lookout State Park** ★★ (© **800/551-6949** or 503/842-4981). Cape Lookout, a steep forested ridge jutting out into the Pacific, is an excellent place for whale watching in the spring. A trail leads out to the end of the point from either the main (lower) parking area or the parking area at the top of the ridge. From the upper parking lot it is a 5-mile round-trip to the point.

South of Cape Lookout, you come to **Pacific City** and **Cape Kiwanda** ★★, the last of the three capes on this scenic loop. Cape Kiwanda, a state natural area, is a sandstone headland backed by a huge sand dune that is popular with hang gliders. It's also fun to climb to the top and then run down. From the top of this giant dune, it is sometimes possible to spot spouting whales. Just offshore is another **Haystack Rock** ★★ every bit as picturesque as the one in Cannon Beach. Because this huge rock breaks the waves, the beach here is used by beach-launched dories, as well as surfers. The

Pelican Pub & Brewery right on the beach here makes a good spot for dinner before heading back to Portland.

From Pacific City, follow signs to U.S. 101 and head north to **Tillamook,** where Ore. 6 heads east toward Portland. Ore. 6 joins U.S. 26 about 25 miles west of Portland. Allow about 2½ hours to get back from Tillamook.

3 A Winery Tour

For many years now, Oregon wines, particularly pinot noirs, have been winning awards. This isn't surprising when you consider that Oregon is on the same latitude as the wine-growing regions of France. The climate is also very similar—cool, wet winters and springs and long, dry summers with warm days and cool nights. These are ideal conditions for growing wine grapes, and local vineyards are making the most of a good situation.

An Oregon winery guide describing more than 70 Oregon wineries is available from the **Oregon Wine Advisory Board,** 1200 NW Naito Pkwy., Suite 400, Portland, OR 97209 (© **503/228-8336;** www.oregonwine.org), or at the **Portland Oregon Visitors Association Information Center,** 1000 SW Broadway, Suite 2300, Portland, OR 97205 (© **877/678-5263** or 503/275-9750; www.travelportland.com).

There are more than two dozen wineries within an hour's drive of Portland. You could easily spend a week getting to know the area's many wineries. However, for an afternoon of wine tasting, we suggest visiting only three or four wineries. A trip through wine country is a chance not only to sample a wide range of wines but also to see the fertile valleys that lured pioneers across the Oregon Trail. We recommend taking along a picnic lunch, which you can of course supplement with a wine purchase. Most wineries have picnic tables, and many of them have lovely views. During the summer, many wineries stage weekend festivals that include live music.

The easiest way to visit the Oregon wine country is to head southwest out of Portland on Ore. 99W. Between the towns of Newberg and Dundee, you'll find about half a dozen wineries right alongside the highway and an equal number tucked into the hills within a few miles of the highway. Along the Ore. 99W, wineries are well marked by official highway department signs. The first winery you'll come to on this route is **Rex Hill Vineyards,** 30835 N. Hwy. 99W, Newberg (© **503/538-0666**); followed by **Duck Pond Cellars,** 23145 Hwy. 99W, Dundee (© **800/437-3213**); **Dundee**

Springs, Hwy. 99W and Fox Farm Rd., Dundee (© **503/554-8000**); **Ponzi Wine Bar,** Hwy. 99W and SW Seventh St., Dundee (© **503/554-1500**); **Argyle,** 691 Hwy. 99w, Dundee (© **503/538-8520**); and **Sokol Blosser,** 5000 Sokol Blosser Lane, Dundee (© **800/582-6668**).

If you opt for this easy, straight-line wine tour, consider stopping for dinner in the town of Dundee, which has several excellent restaurants. **Tina's,** 760 Hwy. 99W (© **503/538-8880**), is a small place with a menu limited to about half a dozen well-prepared dishes. **Red Hills Provincial Dining,** 276 Hwy. 99W (© **503/538-8224**), in an old house beside the highway, serves a combination of Northwest and Mediterranean cuisine. Reservations are highly recommended at both of these restaurants. The **Dundee Bistro,** 100-A SW Seventh St. (© **503/554-1650**), operated by nearby Ponzi Vineyards, serves a wide variety of meals from simple to complex and is affiliated with the adjacent Ponzi Wine Bar.

Alternatively, if you'd like to avoid the crowds and the traffic congestion along busy Ore. 99W, try the wine tour outlined below, which takes in some of the region's best wineries and also some of the most beautiful countryside. To begin this alternative winery tour, head west out of Portland on U.S. 26 (Sunset Hwy.) and then take Ore. 47 south toward Forest Grove.

After a few miles on this two-lane highway, watch for a sign to **David Hill Winery,** 46350 NW David Hill Rd. (© **503/992-8545**). Although the original winery here went out of business during Prohibition, the first grapes were planted on this site in the late 1800s. Today David Hill produces excellent pinot noir and sparkling wines by the *méthode champenoise*. The winery is open March through December Tuesday through Sunday from noon to 5pm.

Continue through Forest Grove on Ore. 47 and just south of town, you'll see a sign for **Montinore Vineyards,** 3663 SW Dilley Rd. (© **503/359-5012**), which has its tasting room in an old Victorian mansion at the top of a tree-lined driveway. This is one of the largest wine producers in the state and enjoys an enviable location with sweeping views across the Tualatin Valley to the Cascade Range. Landscaped grounds invite a stroll or picnic after tasting a few wines. Pinot Noir, Pinot Gris, Chardonnay, and Riesling are among the more popular wines produced here. Between April and December, the winery is open daily from 11am to 5pm; other months, it's open on weekends from 11am to 4pm.

Back on Ore. 47, continue south to the small town of Gaston, where you'll find **24° Brix,** 108 Mill St. (© **503/985-3434**), a combination sandwich shop and wine-tasting room representing several small wineries that are not usually open to the public. About 14 miles south of Gaston on Ore. 47, you'll come to the town of Carlton, which is home to **The Tasting Room,** Main and Pine streets (© **503/852-6733**), another wine-tasting room specializing in wines from wineries that aren't regularly open to the public.

From Carlton, head back north to Gaston, and turn right on East Main Street. In slightly more than a mile turn left at a T-intersection and then turn right on Dixon Mill Road, which turns to gravel. At the end of this road, turn right on Unger Road, which will bring you to **Lion Valley Vineyards,** 35040 SW Unger Rd. (© **503/ 628-5458**), which produces very drinkable, fruit-forward pinot noirs. Open on Saturday and Sunday from noon to 5pm.

From Lion Valley, continue downhill (east) on Unger Road to Ore. 219, turn left, and then turn right onto Burkhalter Road to reach **Oak Knoll Winery,** 29700 SW Burkhalter Rd., Hillsboro (© **503/648-8198**). This winery produces a wide range of wines, including a delicious raspberry dessert wine. From here, continue east on Burkhalter Road, turn right on Rood Bridge Road and then left (east) on Ore. 10 (Farmington Rd.), which will take you to Beaverton, where you can get on Ore. 217 north to U.S. 26 east to Portland.

4 Mount St. Helens National Volcanic Monument

Once it was regarded as the most perfect of the Cascade peaks, a snow-covered cone rising above lush forests, but on May 18, 1980, all that changed. On that day, a massive volcanic eruption blew out the entire north side of Mount St. Helens, laying waste to a vast area and darkening the skies of the Northwest with billowing clouds of ash. Although today the volcano is quiet and life has returned to the once devastated landscape, this volcano and much of the land surrounding it has been designated the Mount St. Helens National Volcanic Monument.

The monument is located roughly 90 miles north of Portland off I-5 (take the Castle Rock exit). Admission to one monument visitor center (or Ape Cave) is $3 ($1 for children 5–15) and to two or more visitor centers (and Ape Cave), is $6 ($2 for children 5–15). If you just want to park at one of the monument's trailheads and go for a hike, all you need is a valid Northwest Forest Pass, which costs $5 per day. If it's winter, you'll need a sno-park Permit ($8 per day).

For more information, contact **Mount St. Helens National Volcanic Monument** (℃ **360/247-3900;** www.fs.fed.us/gpnf/mshnvm).

The best place to start an exploration of the monument is at the **Mount St. Helens Visitor Center** (℃ **360/274-2100**), which is located at Silver Lake, 5 miles east of Castle Rock on Wash. 504. The visitor center houses extensive exhibits on the eruption and its effects on the region. This center is open daily from 9am to 5pm. Before even reaching this center, you can stop and watch a 25-minute, 70mm film about the eruption at the **Mount St. Helens Cinedome Theater** (℃ **877/ERUPTION** or 360/274-9844), which is located at exit 49 off I-5 (tickets $6 adults, $5 seniors and children).

Continuing east from the visitor center, you'll come to the **Hoffstadt Bluffs Visitor Center** (℃ **360/274-7750**) at milepost 27 (open daily 9am–7pm in summer; shorter hours in winter), which has a snack bar and is the takeoff site for 20-minute helicopter flights over Mount St. Helens ($99 with a three-person minimum).

A few miles farther, just past milepost 33, you'll arrive at the **Forest Learning Center** (℃ **360/414-3439**), which is open mid-May through September daily 10am to 6pm and in October daily 10am to 5pm. This is primarily a promotional center for the timber industry, but, in a theater designed to resemble an ash-covered land-scape, you can watch a short, fascinating video about the eruption. There are also displays on how forests destroyed by the blast have been replanted. Outside either of these centers you can usually see numerous elk on the floor of the Toutle River valley far below.

The **Coldwater Ridge Visitor Center** (℃ **360/274-2131**), which is at milepost 47 on Wash. 504, only 8 miles from the crater, is the second of the national monument's official visitor centers. This center features interpretive displays on the events leading up to the eruption and the subsequent slow regeneration of life around the volcano. You'll also find a picnic area, interpretive trail, restau-rant, and boat launch at Coldwater Lake. Hours are late April through late September daily 10am to 6pm, and late September through late April daily 10am to 5pm.

Of all the many visitor centers, none offers a more awe-inspiring view than that from the **Johnston Ridge Observatory** (℃ **360/**

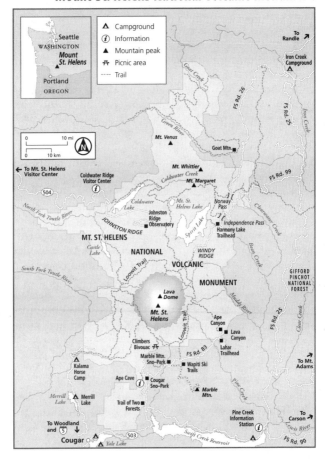

Mount St. Helens National Volcanic Monument

Legend:
- ▲ Campground
- ⓘ Information
- ▲ Mountain peak
- ⼋ Picnic area
- ---- Trail

274-2140), which is located 10 miles past the Coldwater Ridge Visitor Center. Built into the mountainside and designed to blend into the landscape, this observatory houses the equipment that is still used to monitor activity within Mount St. Helens. The observatory is open May through October daily from 10am to 6pm. If you're up for a bit of hiking, the single best trail on this side of the monument is the **Boundary Ridge Trail,** which heads east from the Johnston Ridge Observatory, with a jaw-dropping view of the blast zone the entire way. This trail leads for many miles across the monument, so you can hike as much or as little as you want. There is a good turnaround point about 1 mile out from the observatory.

For a different perspective on the devastation wrought by Mount St. Helens' eruption, drive around to the mountain's east side and the road up to **Windy Ridge.** Although it takes a couple of hours longer to get to this side of the mountain, you'll be rewarded by equaling amazing views, better hiking opportunities, and smaller crowds. To reach the east side of the mountain, take U.S. 12 east from exit 68 off I-5. In Randle, head south on Local Route 25. The **Woods Creek Information Station,** on Route 25 just before the junction with Route 26, has information on this part of the monument.

South of Woods Creek, watch for Route 99, the road to the **Windy Ridge Viewpoint.** This road crosses many miles of blown-down trees, and though the sight of the thousands of trees that were felled by a single blast is quite bleak, it reminds one of the awesome power of nature. More than two decades after the eruption, life is slowly returning to this devastated forest. At the Windy Ridge Viewpoint, visitors get one of the best close-up views of the crater. A staircase of 439 stairs climbs 220 feet up the hill above the parking area for even better views. Below Windy Ridge lies Spirit Lake, which was once one of the most popular summer vacation spots in the Washington Cascades. Today the lake is desolate and lifeless. The 1-mile-long Harmony Trail leads down to the shore of Spirit Lake and is a very worthwhile hike. Just keep in mind that it is a 600-foot climb back up to the trailhead parking lot

If you are an experienced hiker in good physical condition, you may want to consider **climbing to the top of Mount St. Helens.** From the trailhead on the south side of the mountain, it is an 8- to 10-hour, 10-mile hike, and can require an ice ax. Permits ($15) are required April through October, and because this is a very popular climb, it is advisable to make a reservation (© **360/247-3961**). Reservations are taken beginning on February 1, and summer weekends book up fast. However, if you don't have a reservation, you can try your luck by stopping by **Jack's Restaurant and Store** on Wash. 503, 5 miles west of the town of Cougar. Each evening at 6pm this store has a lottery of climbing permits for the next day. Between November 1 and March 31, permits are free and no reservation is necessary, but expect lots of snow.

On the south side of the monument, you can explore the **Ape Cave,** a lava tube that was formed 1,900 years ago when lava poured from the volcano. When the lava finally stopped flowing, it left a 2-mile-long cave that is the longest continuous lava tube in the Western Hemisphere. At the Apes Headquarters (open late May to early Sept), you can join a regular ranger-led exploration of the cave or rent a lantern for exploring the cave on your own.

Hikers who aren't doing the climb to the summit will find many other hiking trails within the monument, some in blast zones and some in forests that were left undamaged by the eruption. Ask at any visitor center for trail information.

Index

See also Accommodations and Restaurant indexes below.

ACCOMMODATIONS

FROMMER'S® COMPLETE TRAVEL GUIDES

Alaska
Alaska Cruises & Ports of Call
Amsterdam
Argentina & Chile
Arizona
Atlanta
Australia
Austria
Bahamas
Barcelona, Madrid & Seville
Beijing
Belgium, Holland & Luxembourg
Bermuda
Boston
Brazil
British Columbia & the Canadian
  Rockies
Budapest & the Best of Hungary
California
Canada
Cancún, Cozumel & the Yucatán
Cape Cod, Nantucket & Martha's
  Vineyard
Caribbean
Caribbean Cruises & Ports of Call
Caribbean Ports of Call
Carolinas & Georgia
Chicago
China
Colorado
Costa Rica
Denmark
Denver, Boulder & Colorado
  Springs
England
Europe
European Cruises & Ports of Call
Florida

France
Germany
Great Britain
Greece
Greek Islands
Hawaii
Hong Kong
Honolulu, Waikiki & Oahu
Ireland
Israel
Italy
Jamaica
Japan
Las Vegas
London
Los Angeles
Maryland & Delaware
Maui
Mexico
Montana & Wyoming
Montréal & Québec City
Munich & the Bavarian Alps
Nashville & Memphis
Nepal
New England
New Mexico
New Orleans
New York City
New Zealand
Northern Italy
Nova Scotia, New Brunswick &
  Prince Edward Island
Oregon
Paris
Philadelphia & the Amish Country
Portugal
Prague & the Best of the Czech
  Republic

Provence & the Riviera
Puerto Rico
Rome
San Antonio & Austin
San Diego
San Francisco
Santa Fe, Taos & Albuquerque
Scandinavia
Scotland
Seattle & Portland
Shanghai
Singapore & Malaysia
South Africa
South America
South Florida
South Pacific
Southeast Asia
Spain
Sweden
Switzerland
Texas
Thailand
Tokyo
Toronto
Tuscany & Umbria
USA
Utah
Vancouver & Victoria
Vermont, New Hampshire &
  Maine
Vienna & the Danube Valley
Virgin Islands
Virginia
Walt Disney World® & Orlando
Washington, D.C.
Washington State

FROMMER'S® DOLLAR-A-DAY GUIDES

Australia from $50 a Day
California from $70 a Day
Caribbean from $70 a Day
England from $75 a Day
Europe from $70 a Day

Florida from $70 a Day
Hawaii from $80 a Day
Ireland from $60 a Day
Italy from $70 a Day
London from $85 a Day

New York from $90 a Day
Paris from $80 a Day
San Francisco from $70 a Day
Washington, D.C. from $80 a Day

FROMMER'S® PORTABLE GUIDES

Acapulco, Ixtapa & Zihuatanejo
Amsterdam
Aruba
Australia's Great Barrier Reef
Bahamas
Berlin
Big Island of Hawaii
Boston
California Wine Country
Cancún
Charleston & Savannah
Chicago
Disneyland®
Dublin
Florence

Frankfurt
Hong Kong
Houston
Las Vegas
London
Los Angeles
Los Cabos & Baja
Maine Coast
Maui
Miami
New Orleans
New York City
Paris
Phoenix & Scottsdale

Portland
Puerto Rico
Puerto Vallarta, Manzanillo &
  Guadalajara
Rio de Janeiro
San Diego
San Francisco
Seattle
Sydney
Tampa & St. Petersburg
Vancouver
Venice
Virgin Islands
Washington, D.C.

FROMMER'S® NATIONAL PARK GUIDES

Banff & Jasper
Family Vacations in the National
  Parks
Grand Canyon

National Parks of the American
  West
Rocky Mountain

Yellowstone & Grand Teton
Yosemite & Sequoia/ Kings Canyon
Zion & Bryce Canyon

FROMMER'S® MEMORABLE WALKS

Chicago
London

New York
Paris

San Francisco
Washington, D.C.

FROMMER'S® GREAT OUTDOOR GUIDES

Arizona & New Mexico
New England

Northern California
Southern New England

Vermont & New Hampshire

SUZY GERSHMAN'S BORN TO SHOP GUIDES

Born to Shop: France
Born to Shop: Hong Kong,
  Shanghai & Beijing

Born to Shop: Italy
Born to Shop: London

Born to Shop: New York
Born to Shop: Paris

FROMMER'S® IRREVERENT GUIDES

Amsterdam
Boston
Chicago
Las Vegas
London

Los Angeles
Manhattan
New Orleans
Paris
Rome

San Francisco
Seattle & Portland
Vancouver
Walt Disney World
Washington, D.C.

FROMMER'S® BEST-LOVED DRIVING TOURS

Britain
California
Florida
France

Germany
Ireland
Italy
New England

Northern Italy
Scotland
Spain
Tuscany & Umbria

HANGING OUT™ GUIDES

Hanging Out in England
Hanging Out in Europe

Hanging Out in France
Hanging Out in Ireland

Hanging Out in Italy
Hanging Out in Spain

THE UNOFFICIAL GUIDES®

Bed & Breakfasts and Country
  Inns in:
  California
  Great Lakes States
  Mid-Atlantic
  New England
  Northwest
  Rockies
  Southeast
  Southwest
Best RV & Tent Campgrounds in:
  California & the West
  Florida & the Southeast
  Great Lakes States
  Mid-Atlantic
  Northeast
  Northwest & Central Plains

Southwest & South Central
  Plains
  U.S.A.
Beyond Disney
Branson, Missouri
California with Kids
Chicago
Cruises
Disneyland®
Florida with Kids
Golf Vacations in the Eastern U.S.
Great Smoky & Blue Ridge Region
Inside Disney
Hawaii
Las Vegas
London

Mid-Atlantic with Kids
Mini Las Vegas
Mini-Mickey
New England and New York with
  Kids
New Orleans
New York City
Paris
San Francisco
Skiing in the West
Southeast with Kids
Walt Disney World®
Walt Disney World® for Grown-ups
Walt Disney World® with Kids
Washington, D.C.
World's Best Diving Vacations

SPECIAL-INTEREST TITLES

Frommer's Adventure Guide to Australia &
  New Zealand
Frommer's Adventure Guide to Central America
Frommer's Adventure Guide to India & Pakistan
Frommer's Adventure Guide to South America
Frommer's Adventure Guide to Southeast Asia
Frommer's Adventure Guide to Southern Africa
Frommer's Britain's Best Bed & Breakfasts and
  Country Inns
Frommer's Caribbean Hideaways
Frommer's Exploring America by RV
Frommer's Fly Safe, Fly Smart
Frommer's France's Best Bed & Breakfasts and
  Country Inns
Frommer's Gay & Lesbian Europe

Frommer's Italy's Best Bed & Breakfasts and
  Country Inns
Frommer's New York City with Kids
Frommer's Ottawa with Kids
Frommer's Road Atlas Britain
Frommer's Road Atlas Europe
Frommer's Road Atlas France
Frommer's Toronto with Kids
Frommer's Vancouver with Kids
Frommer's Washington, D.C., with Kids
Israel Past & Present
The New York Times' Guide to Unforgettable
  Weekends
Places Rated Almanac
Retirement Places Rated